The Toilet Paper
Entrepreneur

The Toilet Paper Entrepreneur

The tell-it-like-it-is guide to cleaning up in business,
even if you are at the end of your roll.

Mike Michalowicz

OBSIDIAN LAUNCH

For information on discounts for bulk purchases, please contact Obsidian Launch at books@obsidianlaunch.com.

Library of Congress Cataloging-in-Publication Data is available.

ISBN-13: 978-0-9818082-8-4

Cover Design by: Salman Salwar
Book Design by: JustYourType.biz

Manufactured in the United States of America

10 9 8 7 6 5 4 3 2 1

DEDICATION

Krista, Tyler, Adayla, & Jake Michalowicz –
Thanks for supporting me unequivocally and
letting me sleep in after the all-nighters on this project.

Success is never the result of one-person endeavors.
Never. It takes a team. Thank you team.
Thank you from the bottom of my heart.

Patty Zanelli, Anjanette Harper, Mini Sankara, Matt Maher,
Scott Bradley, Stephanie Cavataro, Howard Hirsch, Lauren
Lombardo, Sean Moriarty, Lisa Mason, Mike Maddock, Zach
Smith, and everyone who helped in making this book great—
thank you for taking the stones and making a sculpture.
It will never cease to amaze me how much a small, focused,
relentless, passionate group of people can accomplish.

Everyone — We're done for now,
until the masses beg for another book!

(If you are one of the masses,
please feel free to beg for another book.)

CONTENTS

FOREWORD xi

INTRODUCTION xiii

MY THREE-SHEET STORY xix

PART ONE: BELIEFS 1

CHAPTER 1 – NATURE'S CALLING 4
Answer the Urge...4
Obliterate All the Excuses, Except tor One................................9
One Day Still Hasn't Come 14
Nature vs. Nurture...15

CHAPTER 2 – A LITTLE PEACE AND QUIET (IN YOUR MIND).......... 17
How To Blow Your Last $20 on Booze and Still Make Millions 19
The Wall of Limiting Beliefs 21
Envy This.. 24
The Channel of Enabling Beliefs..25
Getting Past Day One..30
Mission I'm Possible..33

CHAPTER 3 – THE FIRE IN YOUR BELLY 36
What To Do? What To Do?..37
What Do You Stand For?...39
Immutable Laws (A Filter for Everything)................................. 41
The Why Guy Finds His Why 47

PART TWO: THE TPE FOCUS.................................49

CHAPTER 4 – GETTING DOWN TO BUSINESS................................... 51
Focus Small To Get Big 52
How To Drive Dangerously Fast, Safely 54
The Focus Five..56
You Gotta Do Better.. 59

Your Area of Innovation – Quality, Price or, Convenience 61
Who's Your Ideal Customer? 64
You Are Really, Really Good At Very, Very Little 67

CHAPTER 5 – IT'S ALL ABOUT REGULARITY 71
A Junk Man's $1B Prosperity Plan 72
Create a Prosperity Plan 74
Always Be Tacking 81
Quarterly Tacking 83
Every Day, Review Your Metrics 88
Gold Bullion Everywhere 92
It's Just Like Driving to Albuquerque 93

PART THREE: ACTION 97

CHAPTER 6 – ARE YOU READY NOW? 99
"No" Your Way to Success 100
The Top Nine List 102
The Dark Side 104
Haven't Been There, Haven't Done That 105
What You Don't Know Can't Pervert You 107
Burn the Boats 109

CHAPTER 7 – SHIT AND GET OFF THE POT 111
The Secret Behind The Secret 112
Just In Case You Haven't Started Yet, Here's How 113
Action, Lights, Camera 116
Happily Walk Out of a Once-in-a-Lifetime Meeting 117
Act As If, But Only on the Inside 119
The 16,107 Steps You (Don't) Need to Take 122
Know When to Say When 124
Accountability 125
A Good Night's Rest in the Hotel Parking Lot 126

PART FOUR: MONEY & EQUITY 129

CHAPTER 8 – CLEAN UP ON THREE SHEETS 131
Plenty of Somethin' from a Whole Lot of Nothin' 132
Anything for Nothing 133

Sometimes You Need To Borrow 135

Bankers Are Anchors 135

Trade a Paperclip for a House 137

Funds from the Folks 139

Vendors Have Your Money. Borrow It Back! (Plus Other Options) ... 140

Don't Borrow To Cover Your Mistakes 143

Don't Give Personal Guarantees 144

CHAPTER 9 – A GOOD, SOLID FLOW 146

Applying the PFA Process to Your Business 148

CHAPTER 10 – KEEP YOUR BUSINESS TO YOURSELF 153

Partners Without Equity 154

Watch Out for VIPs (Very Inordinately Paid Specialists) 156

Ideas Are Worth the Time Spent on Them 157

Angels and VCs Suck (Kinda) 158

The Right Way To Balance Equity & Partnering 159

It's a Big Deal To Be Small 160

Throw Out the Way It Has Always Been 162

BONUS: THE YOUTH (AND YOUNG AT HEART) ADVANTAGE 165

Ivy League or County College – So What! 167

Move In with Your Mom (And Other Painful Thoughts) 169

Master Bocce Ball 169

Still in School? Graduate Profitably. 170

THE NOT-SO-HIDDEN BONUS SECTION: TOM "THE BIG" CRAPPER 173

FOREWORD

So everyone told me I had to get some bigwig to write the foreword to my book. Turns out my book is just a bit too controversial, a bit too blunt, and may have a slight amount of bathroom humor – in other words, no foreword.

But I'm a Toilet Paper Entrepreneur (TPE). I get it done. So I wrote my own damn foreword, which is a crash course in the attributes of the Toilet Paper Entrepreneur — what you must embody if you are going to be one of the people who makes it in business.

Here are my Top Eight TPE Attributes:

1. **The TPE Cultivates a Powerful Foundation of Beliefs** – A TPE knows that success is nearly 100% determined by his or her beliefs, not education, means, or circumstance. When TPEs believe they will achieve something and then back it up with relentless, persistent action, it will happen.

2. **The TPE Has Passion** – A TPE always, unequivocally, works in his or her field of passion. The passion might not be obvious or apparent to an outsider, but it is to the TPE.

3. **The TPE Slants Toward Premature Action** – A TPE will take action over sitting still every time. Taking action too soon may burn them, but inevitably TPEs are rewarded for taking action too early rather than too late.

4. **The TPE Is Extremely Great at Extremely Little** – The TPE discovers his or her few strengths and exploits the

living hell out of them. Whatever he or she sucks at gets outsourced.

5. **The TPE Uses Ingenuity over Money** – Money can be like a drug temporarily covering up all your problems. Money allows you to do stupid things without painful consequences, hence keeping you stupid. The TPE knows that entrepreneurial mastery is determined by ingenuity and a razor-sharp focus.

6. **The TPE Dominates a Niche** – The TPE chooses a market wherein the competition is weak or does not offer the angle of products, services, and values that the TPE can. Then the TPE dominates that niche.

7. **The TPE Marries Long-Term Focus with Short-Term Action** – The TPE knows with absolute certainty where his or her final destination is but doesn't have a detailed play-by-play on how to get there. Instead, TPEs take action in the short term (90 day increments) to make substantial progress. Then they reevaluate their goals, create plans for the next 90 days, and execute them.

8. **The TPE Is NOT Normal** – TPEs are risk takers. They are a little weird and possibly a little crazy. They are definitely different. TPEs do not adhere to rules or abide by social norms. They bust the status quo wide open.

Do you see yourself in this list? If you do, or if you just wish you could, this book is going to rock your world.

INTRODUCTION

*"The world is more malleable than you think
and it's waiting for you to hammer it into shape."*

\- Bono

'm tired…tired of the hundreds, if not thousands, of business books that are all title and no content. Most of those books should be distilled to one or two pages of valuable content. The others should be used to wipe your ass.

I can't tell you how many books I've started poring through and in minutes found myself "boring" through until I finally gave up. Only a select few business books are truly great and need to be read cover to cover.

My goal for *The Toilet Paper Entrepreneur* is to be different and far better than the traditional business books and burned-out grad school rhetoric, from the first word to the last. You'll find no out-dated concepts in this book and no "optimized entrepreneurial execution methodologies." This book is straight from the trenches. I've put all of my effort, experience, and resources into making *The Toilet Paper Entrepreneur* one of the best. You decide if it is.

This book is about getting real, dispelling the naysayers and kicking you in the butt to get up, and do it.

The less you have of something critical, the more important it becomes and the more wisely you use it. This is true with every-thing — love, food, money, and even (or especially) toilet paper.

Have you ever been doing your business with your pants hugging your ankles and, when you are ready to wrap things up, notice that you are extremely low on toilet paper? Don't deny it! You know exactly what I am talking about. Three tattered sheets of TP hang off the edge of the cardboard roll, mocking you.

This is a crappy position to be in (pun intended). There are only two or three options. You could call for help, which is WAY too embarrassing, but is an option. Of course you could do the humbling, hunched shuffle of shame and pray you find a roll somewhere nearby. That's horrible, but it's an option. The final option, usually the best option, is to manage with what you've got. And when you apply your entrepreneurial mind, you quickly recognize you have more than a mere three sheets.

Here's the play-by-play. You go with the final option and decide to manage. Let's be honest: you have a reputation for using more than three sheets. You gotta see what else you can… wait a minute. Ah ha!!! Yes! The wastepaper basket! Like a master gymnast performing a two-handed straddle over a pommel horse, you hold yourself up and stretch your leg out. Just… far… enough. With your leg quivering from the strain, you precariously hook your toes over the garbage pail and start dragging it in. "Come to Momma. Come to Momma," you repeat over and over in your head.

Time to examine your newly found treasure trove: A used snot-rag. Good, very good. A Q-tip. Oh, the inhumanity! Useable, if you must. A few cotton balls. OK, you can work with that. And… dental floss? No way! You draw the line at dental floss. So with three sheets of TP, a few cotton balls, a used tissue and a little poking around with a Q-Tip, you walk out fresh as a daisy ready to face the world. Of course, you don't reload the toilet paper for the next guy. Let him learn the hard way!

The story doesn't end there. The next time you visit the john, you check the TP supply immediately. With a ready supply, you tear through the paper like it is going out of style. Within a few weeks of "the incident," though, you return to your old ways without a fleeting thought of being caught short-handed. Sure enough, before long you get caught again with your pantaloons kissing your ankles and an empty roll, praying you won't need the dental floss this time.

Do you see the amazing entrepreneurial lessons here? In this most challenging, most human moment of all, we demonstrate our infinite ability to pull "miracles" out of the trash. When we literally have no option to just get up and walk away, we find a way to get the job done. With three sheets, some wastebasket scraps and possibly a torn up cardboard roll, the impossible becomes very possible.

It's awe-inspiring how careful, thoughtful, and innovative we are when our supplies are scarce. But it's also confounding how quickly we use and abuse our resources when we perceivably have a lot. The problem is how our heads work. When we have knowledge of abundance in a specific instance (e.g., a full roll of TP), we convert this into a careless perception of perpetual abundance (e.g., an endless supply of TP within arms' reach). Hence, we waste what we have. Even worse, we don't check to make sure it isn't running out. We just assume it's going to be there. We sit down, do our business, and THEN grab thin air. Damn! Here we go again.

Now, what if every time you sat down there were only three sheets of toilet paper left on the roll? When you always expect scant resources, you quickly get in the habit of being very careful in your cleanup, every time. You sure as hell would ensure the garbage basket was in your lap before you got rolling. You may even adjust your behaviors to preserve what you have, possibly making other "stops" before you got home or eating more rice or something. Your mindset, your focus, and your actions would all change in anticipation of having less to work – or wipe – with.

Your success is completely determined by your ability to break free from the one and only approach everyone else is following. Your success is completely determined by how you use your mind, how you manage your critical resources, and how decisively you act to achieve the "impossible" with very few traditional resources. Your success is completely determined not by giving up and waiting for some extra rolls, but by going with what you've got. The people who elect to master this knowledge and exploit it in their business are the few, the proud, the Toilet Paper Entrepreneurs!

The Toilet Paper Entrepreneur Is Not for Common-Thinking People

The Toilet Paper Entrepreneur is not for the faint of heart (or for those with an intolerant colon, for that matter). This book is for people who have a desire to achieve entrepreneurial success, know it's gonna be tough, and have the guts to stick it out. It's not for the wannabes and the talkers. This book is NOT for people who are willing to "try" something new simply to identify all the "problems" and therby prove that they were right in the first place. You know who you are. And this book is definitely not for people who think a single book or a series of materials can take them from rags to riches.

This book is for people who want to challenge the status quo. This book is for people who will take lessons, use them to exploit their strengths, and then go for it with all they've got. Most importantly, this book is for people who take sole responsibility for their own success or failure. Success in business isn't about being right; it's about being committed. So, do you want to be right or do you want to be successful? I pick success.

Your Success Is Up to You

The safety of a lifelong career with a large company died out long ago with one final dying Enron gasp. The security, the fun, and all the rewards exist in entrepreneurialism. Think about it: You can't trust or depend on anyone more than yourself. And I am willing to bet that you already have all the skills you need to get started – you probably just need a better awareness of what you already have, as well as a swift kick in the ass. That's my job.

It's time you hear the truth and not some sugarcoated nonsense or formula for quick success. Launching and building a company is freaking hard. It is scary, time-consuming, frustrating, and sometimes life-draining. And, quite frankly, you might fuck it up and ruin yourself financially. But financial disaster is unlikely if you relentlessly commit to your own success. If you exploit your strengths, you can create a company that feeds your wallet and your soul, a company that exhilarates and frees you. If you have the destination, this book is the map.

The thing I can't do is travel for you. You must be willing to try something new, push beyond your perceived limitations, and grow. The responsibility for your entrepreneurial experience sits squarely on your shoulders. The meek may inherit the earth one day, but they sure as hell won't be entrepreneurs.

Having been down the road of building three companies of my own from scratch, partnering in the launch of many others, and researching hundreds of other startups, I have discovered commonalities among successful company launches, which I outline in this book. I'll tell you one thing right off, it sure isn't common thinking. So ignore what you were told in business school, forget what you think you know about startups, and throw out your dad's method of money management. There is a new generation of entrepreneurs, and it is time for a new *modus operandi*.

Are you ready to get off the pot?

MY THREE-SHEET STORY

Facebook, Google, and YouTube all rocketed to incredible success faster than you can say the words "holy sheet." They are worth hundreds of millions, or billions, or hundreds of billions. The surprising thing is that the founders were all twenty-somethings when they launched AND made their gazillions. Holy sheet! Their success is amazing and for that they get the lion's share of media attention. They are heralded as the best of the best and the foundation of the new economy.

My experience was different. Way different. And the main difference between my story and those of the "Media Darling Entrepreneurs" (MDEs) is *how* we launched and built our businesses, but we'll get to all of that later. The successes of the Toilet Paper Entrepreneurs are rarely discussed, let alone heralded in the media. Yet it is these "everyday" entrepreneurs who are slowly but surely marching along, creating amazing companies and achieving remarkable results.

Google is not "real" in that it is not a typical experience. However, its success is achievable for your own business if you truly believe it (more on that later). But Google should not be seen as *the* path to success, simply as one path.

There are many other paths traveled by the likes of the well-known and the unknown. These are the paths of the TPEs. Some of them are well-known, such as Bill Hewlett & David Packard, who started their company with $538 and a garage workshop, ultimately yielding today's $100 billion conglomerate; some of them are somewhat lesser-known entrepreneurs like Brian Scudamore of 1-800-GOT-JUNK? who took a summer dream and turned it into a junk business now approaching $200 million in revenue. Dave Packard, Bill Hewlett, and Brian Scudamore are all Toilet Paper Entrepreneurs. So am I. And, I expect, so are you.

I am here to tell you their stories and the stories of others as well as the lessons learned. I am here to tell you the real deal of successful entrepreneurship. It is bloated with failures, drenched with progress, marred with mistakes, and peppered with major achievements.

So who am I to talk about this stuff? I am a Toilet Paper Entrepreneur. My journey was a fight in the trenches, but I learned how to get out and make it big. Often funny, sometimes a struggle, my entrepreneurial adventure has been far from glamorous. I even moved my wife and infant into a retirement village to save money – nothin' glamorous there, believe me. Unless you like shuffleboard and funky-smelling old people.

And I have found myself stranded on the toilet bowl once or twice. I've worked forty-eight hours straight because I had to, sleeping in clients' conference rooms to save on hotel bills. And as I write this I'm sitting at a used desk I scavenged to save bucks, even though I have more than enough dough to swing a trip to Office Depot.

The odds are that your path will be more like mine than Mark Zuckerberg's of Facebook. But I want you to know that success can be achieved following any path. You don't need to have a "full roll" to walk out winning; you can do it with just three sheets of TP. And no matter which path you choose, you have to do it with strong beliefs, absolute focus, and loads of effort.

Here's a quick look at my three-sheet story vs. the MDEs:

MEDIA DARLING ENTREPRENEUR	MIKE'S "THREE SHEET" PATH
Age 6 - Starts a lawn mowing business by recruiting teenagers in the neighborhood. Buys parents a house.	**Age 6** - Still in diapers.
Age 12 - Sits on the board of major toy company.	**Age 12** - Rushed to a major hospital for eating a toy.
Age 18 - Is recruited by top Ivy League schools but rejects them to launch a VC-funded company.	**Age 18** - Picks a college based upon the favorable guy-to-girl ratio. Arrives and is instantly rejected by the girls.
Age 19 - Masters the management of a multi-million-dollar company.	**Age 19** - Masters the inverted keg tap.
Age 21 - Goes public.	**Ages 21** - Goes home.
Age 24 - Retires.	**Age 24** - Drinks too many beers and starts own company because "any idiot can do it."
Age 24 and 1 day - Comes out of retirement. Celebrations ensue.	**Age 24 and 1 day** - Launches a new company, finds out that any idiot cannot do it. Panic ensues.
Age 27 - Has another super success because everyone expects it.	**Age 27** - Company succeeds because there is no alternative.
Age 30 - Is no longer in the news because the next 18-year-old phenom is all over the headlines.	**Age 30** - Finds his passion, launches another company, grows fast and strong.
Age 33 - Seeks psychiatric help to "find himself."	**Age 33** – Found himself! Is living his passion. Business and life are great.
Age 36 - Writes book on life story. Doesn't sell. Goes to work for a TPE.	**Age 36** – Inspires a new breed of business leaders – the TPEs. TPEs go on to hire failed MDEs.

So what are my successes? I have the list of obligatory accomplishments, but more importantly, I have discovered my passion and am living it! I love launching startup businesses, making them great, and doing it fast. I love the underdog, the unsung hero, the people who are committed to their goals but maybe aren't given a fair chance. I love helping people even out the odds, showing them how to exploit their natural strengths so they can go out and kick ass. My life's vocation is all about working hand-in-hand with first-time entrepreneurs to grow their concepts into industry leaders. I love doing this. As a result, I am extremely happy, making a great living and feel constantly energized. I have achieved health, wealth, and happiness all at once. To me, this is my greatest success. What will yours be?

My List of Obligatory Accomplishments

In case you don't want to Google my ass, here are my resume highlights:

I started my first business, a computer integration company, at twenty-four. I sold the company on December 31, 2002, through a private transaction. It lives on today as a thriving company.

On January 1, 2003, I started a new company. Yes, the very next day. That company came into national prominence in three short years and was subsequently acquired by a large public firm in 2006.

I started my third company, Obsidian Launch, in the summer of 2005. The name was different back then, and so was the preliminary concept. It changed because I took time to look introspectively, discover what I really loved to do, and slowly build the concept around my interests and life goals. My earlier companies, while very successful, were built on concepts that were desirable to the market but didn't exploit my talents and my passion to their fullest. My latest company has all that covered, so I'm good.

I have followed the path of the Toilet Paper Entrepreneur, early on unintentionally and unaware, but over time deliberately and with stronger focus. Throughout, I have valued my beliefs, discovered and exploited my strengths, and, most importantly, never stopped pushing ahead, even during the toughest times. The results?

In addition to selling two companies for lots of cash;

- I now partner in the launch of a new company approximately every four weeks;

- I am a reccurring guest on *The Big Idea with Donny Deutsch* and other television programs;

- I have received many entrepreneur awards, including the SBA's Young Entrepreneur of the Year Award;

- I have been interviewed in many national media outlets;

- I have presented at some of this country's most prestigious universities (and I barely had a B average at Virginia Tech – go figure);

- I am the author of this book and intend to write many more;

- And, most importantly, I continue to quickly grow revenue and profits for all my companies!

My goal is not to be a braggart here but simply to point out that if I can do this, so can you. Also, make sure you don't mix up getting media exposure with being a Media Darling. Exposure in the media is a great thing – I strongly suggest you seek it out, as I do. Being an MDE is something different than mere exposure; it is more about the overnight successes who *actually do* achieve success over night. MDEs should be an exalted group, no question. But they should not be perceived as an exclusive group.

You can and will achieve success, too, if you want. Your overnight success may just take time to build. Ultimately you can achieve any goals you desire, and you can do it all by following the path of the Toilet Paper Entrepreneur.

Clearly I have not followed the path of the MDE, but most entrepreneurs don't. You too will most likely launch your business with three sheets, a wing, and a prayer. My job is to help you get rid of the wing and prayer part. Your job is to succeed on your three sheets.

Let's get started, shall we?

PART ONE:

Beliefs

"God didn't have time to make a nobody, only a somebody. I believe that each of us has God-given talents within us waiting to be brought to fruition."

— Mary Kay Ash

At the start of my presentations I use the old Jack Canfield demonstration, the one with the $100 bill. It goes something like this:

I start out by asking, "Who here wants to be a multi-millionaire?" A room full of hands go up. "Who here IS a multi-millionaire?" The hands go down. "Who wants to have a positive impact on this world?" Hands go up. "Who has accomplished it?" Hands go down. "Who wants to be known for the good they did?" Hands up. "Who has achieved this?" Hands down.

After I explain to the attendees that these are all inspiring aspirations but are truly unattainable in this one moment, I fish through my pocket, pull out a $100 bill and hold it up. I say, "This is something we can all see and talk about. Who wants this $100 bill?" All the hands go up. I ask again, "Who wants the $100 bill?" The hands stay up, accompanied by strange looks. The third time I ask, I get the same response. Often it takes four or five times before one person sheepishly gets out of his chair, walks over and cautiously takes the $100 bill from my hand. The rest of the audience looks stupefied.

When the $100 guy returns to his seat, we go through an exploration of our beliefs. Even though all raised their hands saying they wanted the money, their beliefs prevented them from taking it. The beliefs are always the same: "It's a trick;" "It's embarrassing;" "You'll just take it back;" "Someone else deserves it." These powerful limiting beliefs keep everyone's butt stuck to the seat, even though each wants the $100.

But that one person, maybe out of pure frustration, elected to change his beliefs. "I'm going to go for it." "What's the worst that can happen?" "So what if it is a trick, at least it will be over." "Maybe I can just take it." "Maybe it's not a trick. I'm going for it, now!"

The only thing between the audience and that $100 bill is air. There is nothing else, yet the forces of their beliefs are so powerful that they are literally immobilized. I wonder how many $100 bills and other opportunities they regularly miss out on because of fear.

Imagine yourself at that presentation. I bet you would have raised your hand like everyone else, stating you wanted or planned to be a millionaire. But like everyone else, I bet you wouldn't have grabbed the money from me. If you aren't going to get out of your seat to take a $100 bill, what in the world makes you think you will do anything to make $100 mil? You won't.

You can't do anything if you don't have the beliefs to back it up. And don't try to fool yourself and say it will be different when the stakes are higher and that then you would do whatever it takes to make millions. If you can't get yourself to grab the first $100 toward your millions when it is literally waved in your face, what makes you think you will behave any differently in business? If you are going to succeed, you need to destroy your limiting beliefs and create enabling beliefs.

About forty-five minutes into my presentation I do a wrap-up that ties back to the opening demonstration. I tell the attendees I can prove that they all have in fact changed their beliefs. I reach back into my pocket and hold up another $100 bill. Before I can say a word everyone makes a mad dash toward me, and in an instant the money is gone. That's the power of an enabling belief. Your entrepreneurial success depends on it.

CHAPTER 1 – NATURE'S CALLING

"To succeed, we must first believe that we can."
- Michael Korda

Two great warriors are about to fight. One of the warriors volunteered because of his undying love for his country; the other was simply paid handsomely to fight. Which one would you bet on?

Always bet on the individual who is serving his calling, not the guy who is doing it for the money. It is the person who is serving his purpose and fulfilling his heart's desire who will see his business through the good times and the bad. Those that are following their path will relentlessly march forward during the ups and downs, even as others give up to pursue something else. They will be there when the paid guys walk away. If you try to get rich by doing the next big thing, but it isn't your passion, the competitor who really is passionate about it will eat you up and spit you out. Passion begets persistence. And persistence begets success.

Answer the Urge

For you to launch a dominant business, you must first find what you thirst for. This took me years to discover. When I started out I had this belief that entrepreneurs should do what they know, not what they want. I knew computers and liked working on them, so I launched a business related to that. But I didn't *love* computers. It

TPE TIP

The Business – While not the best form of legal protection, Sole Proprietorship is a cheap way of getting started, since there are no setup costs. There are fees associated with setting up an S-Corp, C-Corp and limited liability corporation (LLC). Of course, as you make money you will need to pay taxes just like anyone else, and you will want to incorporate down the road. Consult with an accountant (not one you pay for, but one who is a qualified expert from a local college) on next steps. An LLC is often the most economical and effective way to go.

was my vocation, not my passion. My first two businesses were successful, but not because I was passionate about technology. I didn't eat, sleep, and breathe tech.

But I loved entrepreneurialism. I could talk about business all day, read every magazine, attend every seminar, and still my thirst would not be quenched. It took me a few years to figure out what was sitting right under my nose the entire time: That I loved launching businesses. Once I came to the realization that it is the birthing and maturing of a business that I love, I knew the path my future would follow.

It doesn't have to take years to discover what really gets you jazzed. The key is to reflect and take the time now, rather than figure it out through trial and error.

What would you volunteer to do simply because of your love for it? What activities bring you the most happiness, energy and satisfaction? What makes you lose track of time, complete tasks almost effortlessly, and come out even more energized? When you are talking with friends, what is the one subject you can just go on and on and on about, until they are rolling their eyes? Answer these questions and you've found your heart's desire. And when you have found your insatiable thirst, your passion, you will have taken the most important step to launching a company that will excel.

Perhaps you've had a fleeting thought of starting a business, or maybe you are on fire with ideas and ready to jump in full swing. Either way, you need to get started by stopping. No, that's not a typo. The best response to a waterfall of what-if dreams is a deep, thought-provoking breath. A successful launch is more about you and your beliefs than anything else. Committing to a business without intimately knowing yourself is a fool's dream. Going "all-in" on a bad hand is a stupid move, and so is jumping feet-first into business without knowing the cards you're holding.

To get started at launching your company or to clean up a mediocre start, you must begin by discovering yourself. You need to understand and acknowledge your heart's desire, your mindset, and beliefs. You need to lead with introspective thought. You need to learn all about what you're all about.

Just for a minute, if there were no limits to what is possible, what would you envision your entrepreneurial company providing you? The first thing that pops into almost everyone's mind is financial independence. I agree. I totally agree. But there is more, isn't there? What if building your business made you feel emotionally satisfied, totally happy? What if your business made a difference? What if you woke up every morning excited to work? What if people loved your company? What if the world heralded what you did and happily consumed what you had to offer?

Owning a business is NOT about working your ass off for the sake of trying to squeeze out a living. It is NOT about making tons of money at the expense of losing tons of life. It IS about maximizing life, bettering your life and the lives of others, which, not so ironically, fattens your purse.

The greatest example of work-your-ass-off business ownership came from the quintessential entrepreneur himself, Sam Walton, founder of Wal-Mart. Walton started a company based upon a simple dream and went on to become one of the richest men in the world. The lesson? "I blew it." Those are the words Walton reportedly voiced from his deathbed. By his own measures he was a failure – a billionaire who barely knew his youngest child and was married to a woman who stayed with him for reasons short of a fulfilling relationship.

What final words would you like to utter? I hope they are words steeped with feelings of contentment, words that say that you lived life to the fullest, pushed beyond your limits, and built a company that you are proud of both for how much it accomplished and for how much it made.

If this is the type of success you want, you can have it. It all starts and ends with you. It doesn't start with where the market is headed. It doesn't start with the latest and greatest trends. It doesn't even start with what you believe the customers want. Your business starts with you.

Yesterday's financially-fat companies were able to market their way out of a crap product. If they ran enough late-night television ads and made big, albeit false, claims in the magazines, they were guaranteed tons of customers. Disappointed customers, but customers nonetheless.

That was then and this is now. Today's successful businesses are growing because they are truly great. They are providing unmatched services and products, and the word is getting out, virally. No longer can you count on a marketing budget alone to bring loads of customers. Today you need to provide unmatched services and products. The marketing is done virally – at summer barbeques, in Internet forums, and on perpetual blogs. It's that simple. And for you to provide the best that you imaginably can, it needs to come from both your head and your heart. When your company comes from your soul, when your company is all about you, it becomes a formidable force.

Years ago a major corporation invited me to speak to a group of about forty marketing specialists that sold an insurance product and were trying to break into the small business market. They wanted to learn how to "speak" to the entrepreneur. The presentation was scheduled to start at 9 a.m., but we couldn't get started until 9:20 because everyone was late.

I started by asking them who woke up that morning excited to come to work. The few who raised their hands clearly did it for political posturing, not out of sincerity. Then I asked who loved their job so much that they came in an hour early to work, not because they had to but because they wanted to. All of them scoffed at me. I then explained that for this meeting I had arrived at 7 a.m., just to make sure I found the building and was ready to go. I then had breakfast next door and walked in twenty minutes early to set up.

TPE TIP

Web Presence – Every business needs a web presence, right? Absolutely. But that doesn't mean you need a website. Those are two very different things. You can establish a web presence by using Facebook.com, MySpace.com, Squidoo.com or a million other social sites. Spread the word about what you are doing through these social sites and set up free email. Supplement your social networking site with a free blog at Blogspot.com. That's more than enough to get some business rolling in.

In this one example I have explained the difference between an entrepreneur driven by passion and someone who just has a job. When we love what we do, we do it to our heart's content, and we naturally excel. I arrived at the presentation early not because I needed to but because I *wanted* to. I love entrepreneurialism, and the opportunity to discuss it drives me to be ready to roll, day and night.

Obliterate All the Excuses, Except for One

"Excuses are like assholes. Everyone has one, and they all stink." I don't know who came up with this quotation, but I have a feeling I would really like the guy. Excuses are a great mechanism to apply logic to our fears. They are simply the machinations we go through to defend our inner fears. I have heard and experienced them all. And they are all B.S. All, that is, except one, but I'll save that one for last.

The economy is not strong enough to start a business – Everyone is experiencing the same economy as you are, so you are on equal footing. If the economy is in a recession, buyers may slow down their activity, but competitors will also fall by the wayside. A weak economy is like a forest fire; it kills off many of the plants, but the seeds that take hold now have the most room to grow as the forest comes back to life. A weak economy is often the best time to start.

Entrepreneurship is very risky – Anything that you go into without preparation and knowledge is risky. So go in prepared! The funny thing is, you are already mostly prepared and don't even know it. If you listen to your inner emotion, your calling, you will naturally be led down a path where you already have strengths. You probably have mastered many of the critical learning steps, and you'll pick up all the new stuff like a sponge.

A job with a big company is far more secure – Tell that to the folks who got fired from Enron, Arthur Anderson, Bear Sterns, or any of the other hundreds of large companies that have collapsed or downsized. When you work for someone else, you can be fired at whim. If he screws up, you pay. When you work for yourself, you can't get fired, and the only limit to your success is you.

I'm too old to start a company – So what are you going to do about it? Wait until you are younger? There is no time like the present. Life has yet to offer a rewind or a redo. Don't live with regrets. Get started now, regardless of your age. The self-discovery process you will go through creating your new company is well worth it. Plus, you can leave a little inheritance to the next generation.

I am too young to start a company – What?!?! Did you know that you could legally start and incorporate your own business at any age?

You can literally start your own company before you can legally work for someone else. One of my friends, Cameron Johnson, started his first business at age seven and incorporated his first company by age twelve. Why don't you be the first to start a business at age six? No matter how old or how young you are, start today!

I won't make enough money – A recent study by the National Association of Colleges and Employers (NACE) stated that the average starting salary for an Accounting major is $46,292. Not bad. If you took that job and received an annual raise of 10% each year for the next ten years, you'd be making $120,069. Not bad at all. Now if you start your own company, your salary the first year will average $50,000 according to World Wide Learn. Not bad either. If you run your company well and you elect to give yourself a 25% raise every year (I give myself an average of a 50% raise every year), on your tenth anniversary you will be earning $465,661. Now *that's* sweet!

I don't have the proper education – If you feel you need a college degree to succeed, you are sorely mistaken. I've met with Ph.D.s from Harvard and dropouts from high school; their entrepreneurial successes were directly tied to their beliefs, desire, passion, and thirst to learn through the school of hard knocks. Your scholastic pedigree has basically no influence on your success. None!

I don't have enough money to start – That's great! If you had enough money to "properly" launch your company, I would fear you might go bankrupt. The fact that you have no money (or very little) simply means you need to apply your head right from the get go. There is a reason they say necessity is the mother of invention. Money covers up problems and weaknesses. Without money, you've got to bring your A-game every day. Lack of funds forces you to optimize everywhere and grow the right way.

The competition is too strong – My mother always told me that no two people are alike. She was right. If you think the competition can do a better job than you ever can, then you aren't properly positioned to exploit your strengths. Find an angle to apply your strengths, your innate talents, and your passion in a way that no one else is doing, or no one else is doing well.

No one will buy my product or service – Good thing you caught that now, but it's not an excuse not to launch a company. It simply means you need to reinvestigate what you want to do and determine a new way of delivering it so that you can build a customer base.

I am not ready – I agree; you're not. You never will be. This excuse is simply a combination of all the others. When I ask people why they think they're not ready, they resort to some semblance of one of the other excuses listed. They are all nonsense. Go time is now!

I am sure you can think of many other creative excuses not to start a business. You need to put these rationalizations aside, look ahead, and take action now. We rarely regret the things we did in life when we have followed our passion and taken risks. Too often, though, we regret the things we didn't do. If your heart is calling you to take action, don't use any one of these excuses to squash your desire.

There is one reason not to start a business. Don't start a business if your reason is simply to get rich quick. Greed is not becoming and does not have lasting results. No matter when you are presented with barrels full of money, you DO pay for them. Even if you collect your money prior to any effort, like a lottery winner, for example, nature still has an uncanny way of making you earn it. If you're lucky, your windfall may be earned through the rapid mastery of a new financial discipline. But all too often the earning comes in the form of despair, disaster, and bankruptcy.

Just look at what happens to some big lottery winners – it isn't pretty. Jack Whittacker sure wished he'd torn his lotto ticket up. A TPE, he had plugged away for years, building a construction company that grossed $16 million a year. But after Jack won $315 million, his life became total hell. He lost friends, family, and had four hundred legal claims against him. I'm not trying to talk doom and gloom here; I am just trying to point out that getting rich quick rarely happens, is not satisfying, and in some cases has disastrous results.

Quick money is very alluring. It is rare to meet someone who isn't dying to win the lottery or receive some windfall of cash. Most people, of course, never get a dime wishing for a big payout. It is a shame that the majority of us waste even a second of life hoping something will be handed to us instead of using our talents and passion to make it ourselves.

Money is an amplifier of habits. If you have bad habits and receive lots of money, you will simply repeat your bad habits more often. If your habits are good, it will amplify those good behaviors. Money allows us to be more of who we already are. So we better have a strong mindset and have established good habits before we get gobs of money. When you have achieved a strong, focused, happy mind and are executing on good habits, money will come easily. And money will build more money. And good habits will grow. Happiness, too. That is the healthy way to get rich.

Launch a company to get rich right, not to get rich quick. It works.

TPE TIP

Product Sales – You don't need an ecommerce site when eBay has already created one for you. While not free, this is a really inexpensive way of getting your products into the hands of consumers. And you don't have to auction off product; you can set up an eBay store where you sell things at fixed prices. There are also a number of niche auction sites out there, so start searching!

One Day Still Hasn't Come

If I only had a nickel for every time I heard an aspiring entrepreneur say, "One day." One day I will launch a company. One day I will be this, one day I will do that. Would someone please tell me what the date is for "one day?" Because it sure as hell isn't posted anywhere on my calendar!

It is now or never. One day is a dream. One day is a hope that if everything magically falls into place, success will land in your lap. So if you are at all serious about launching your first company, put an actual date on "one day." Is it one month from now, six months, a year? Tell everyone close to you the day you will be opening the doors of your new company. Then back-calculate all the things that you need to do, back to today, back to this moment right now, and start taking action. NOW!!! Maybe it is setting up a phone line or establishing an LLC or taking a class. The key is to start doing it now and don't stop.

Oh yeah, I almost forgot. Tell your biggest, smelliest, hairiest, zit-ridden friend that you need him to keep you accountable to your goal of starting your first company. Promise him that if you miss this goal, you will let your friends take a picture of you kissing his naked keester and allow it to be posted all over the Internet. If that doesn't get you in gear, I don't know what will.

Nature vs. Nurture

I find it laughable, the amount of time experts spend debating the entrepreneurial nature vs. nurture argument. Let's settle this once and for all: IT'S NATURE. No one can teach you to have entrepreneurial passion. You can't learn how to grow a burning, unquenchable desire for business. No one can train your attitude or make you intelligent. This is all stuff that nature has either given you or hasn't.

You better have the entrepreneurial bug in you or you'll struggle to have even a modicum of success. You can water the soil all you want, but you won't grow a tree unless there is a seed first. If you have it naturally, then it can be nurtured into something great.

There is an important thing to note about nature; it doesn't always present itself at birth or even in the early years. Sometimes your natural thirst for entrepreneurialism beats out of your chest when you're twenty years old. Other people don't feel it until they are collecting social security. Me? It took four cold ones at the local bar. Regardless of when the urge presents itself, when you feel it, go for it. Nature's calling. Answer it.

TAKE ACTION NOW!

Small steps lead to big gains. At the end of each chapter you'll find three action steps you can complete in under half an hour. So you have no excuse!

1. What's your heart's desire? What gets you totally juiced up, so much so that you think you could be happy doing it every day? Write it down in as much detail as possible, paying attention to what you *really* get out of it. Sometimes we think we want something tangible when really we want to feel a certain way or experience something over and over again.

2. Make a list of every single excuse you have used to put off starting your business. If you're already operating a business, write down other little lies you tell yourself that keep you from your heart's desire.

3. Debunk your list of excuses. Write down every reason why your excuse doesn't ring true. If you're really feeling pumped, convert your excuse into a positive statement about your abilities.

CHAPTER 2 – A LITTLE PEACE AND QUIET (IN YOUR MIND)

"My music will go on forever. Maybe it's a fool who say that,
but when me know facts me can say facts.
My music will go on forever."
— Bob Marley

A belief is the thought behind the thought. Profound! A belief is not simply something said with confidence, although that is part of it. A belief is not something repeatedly stated, although that can influence it. A belief is not something you commit to do, albeit it helps. A belief is what your inner emotion is telling you. A belief is the inner, unswayable knowledge of what you know to be true. It's that constant, ever-present conversation that is going on in your head.

Here is the problem. You are constantly lying to yourself through your words and thoughts, and sometimes you even temporarily persuade yourself, but it doesn't last for long. Until you start recognizing and managing that inner, indescribable emotion, you are not going to make sustained progress.

A classic example is someone who is trying to lose weight. You know the people I am talking about: they go on a quick-fix diet and lose lots of weight, only to gain it back plus some months later. They fail at their goal of long-term weight loss because of limiting beliefs, fleeting focus, and sporadic and depleting actions. Without a foundation of enabling beliefs, focus will not be sustained nor action be accomplished. For people to lose weight, they must believe not only that they *can* drop the pounds but also that they *will* drop the pounds. They need to viscerally know that a healthy body involves a lifelong life-style change and believe they *must* live that way. Weight loss is more about what goes on in your head than anything else. Actually, any accomplishment is more about your beliefs than anything else.

Just because you believe something doesn't mean it is actually true. You might think so. Others may not. Who's right? Neither and both. See, it doesn't matter if there even is a "real" truth; what matters is what you believe the truth to be. We are hardwired to behave in absolute consistency with our own beliefs. Our emotions act like an invisible GPS system and move us toward our beliefs every time without fail.

"I believe I should be a millionaire," you say, "but I'm not, so your idea is stupid and you're dead wrong." After I stick my tongue out at you, I explain that you have already achieved your belief. You SHOULD be a millionaire, but you aren't because you believe only that you should be and don't believe that you are. Your inevitable response is, "OK, I believe I AM a millionaire and I am still not." And my response is "Liar!!! You don't really believe that you are, therefore, you aren't." Your final comment is, "Of course I don't believe it, because I am not." And because you don't believe it you aren't.

Until you believe something to be absolutely true, just as you believe the sky is blue and the sun makes light, you won't be able to realize it. Sorry, but that's how it works. It's time you start being extremely cognizant of your beliefs and using them to achieve your desires.

This is not about lying to yourself. That simply doesn't work. It is about aligning all your beliefs, focus, and action to be consistent with your desires. When you do this your beliefs will manifest in money, success, and whatever else you desire. The bad news is that changing beliefs is hard. But this is the foundational component to entrepreneurial success, and without supportive beliefs you will not achieve any degree of success.

Here's the good news. Beliefs can be changed! To establish a new belief you will need to have congruency between your gut and your head. To get there you first need to understand the two types of beliefs that exist, limiting and enabling. Then you need to decide, in your head, what your new belief is. Finally, you need to allow your gut to adjust, accept, and commit to the new belief.

Every Toilet Paper Entrepreneur knows that if you want success, you have to get your beliefs in check. You have to know that you will succeed, regardless of the challenge in front of you. A consistent, enabling frame of mind and the guts to get it done will make all the difference. A mismatching of mind and gut will stop you dead in your tracks.

How To Blow Your Last $20 on Booze and Still Make Millions

A few months after arriving from England in search of the American Dream, David Tyreman was down to his last $20. Just as his former boss predicted, his business idea – selling antiques to Americans via living room parties – had failed. You probably think you know what David did next. You're thinking this is a story about how he took $20 and turned it into millions.

Wrong. David and his business partner blew their last $20 at a bar. (They are from England, after all.) What the hell, right? Might as well have a little fun while you're going down with the ship. But the next morning, David realized he had experienced his worst nightmare – total failure – and it wasn't so bad. Nobody died; the earth didn't open up and swallow him whole.

So he decided to try again. Over the next few months David changed his business model, targeting retail stores that needed antiques for merchandise displays. Even though he knew nothing about his industry and had a tough competitor that dominated the market, he found a way to get his first few clients.

Unlike his competitor, David stored his inventory in a garage, recruiting his friends to help him deliver the merchandise. Without a fat bankroll, he built his business using sweat and ingenuity. David had to think outside the box, which turned out to be exactly what his clients wanted. He realized retailers were using his antiques for differentiation, and that he was not in the antique business but the brand identity business. This realization would make him millions.

David leveraged his success by transforming his company from London Antique, a visual merchandising company, to Propaganda, a branding company that sold antiques *and* a wide range of items retailers needed for branding. It was a huge step, but David wasn't afraid of failure. And when Polo's Ralph Lauren came calling, looking for a new branding company, David took the leap. Did he know how Propaganda would meet the demand? No. Did he worry about it? Not so much. So what if he failed?

Within just a few years David's company, Propaganda, landed other huge clients such as Banana Republic, Old Navy, and Nike. After years of thinking creatively and boldly, David had become a branding expert. He later sold his multi-million dollar company and formed World Famous, a company that helps people and companies develop a brand identity – one of the most valuable assets a business has.

David took chances in part because he wasn't afraid of failure. He no longer believed failure was the worst thing that could happen to him. He'd been there and done that, and he knew better. David Tyreman is a Toilet Paper Entrepreneur.

The Wall of Limiting Beliefs

Business is all about departing from your current plateau, point (A), with the intent of getting to your next achievement, point (B). Maybe you want to start selling your first service offering. Currently your sales are at $0; that is (A). You want to have your sales at $400,000 by the end of the year, that's (B). If you have limiting beliefs they will establish a wall. The wall will block your progress and may even cause you to take other directions that might make things worse.

For this example, let's assume you have limiting beliefs that include:

1. You have no money and without it you can't market your product.

2. You have never done this before, so the competition will easily beat you.

3. You are too young to be respected by the business community.

4. No one has ever been able to grow sales that fast in your industry. It just can't be done.

Now let's look at each of these beliefs and how they can derail entrepreneurial dreams:

1. **You Can't Market Products without Money** – I've seen people squash great ideas for products simply because they think they don't have enough money to market them. Or worse, they put less time and money into making a *great* product in order to reserve funds for marketing, which results in a mediocre product backed by inadequate marketing. A sure prescription for disaster. If a product is great, it will market itself. Believe that your marketing can be done for free or cheaply (it can). As the product sells, cash will become available to further push sales.

2. **The Competition Will Beat Your Inexperienced Ass** – Again, a belief like this almost always results in inaction. Even worse, people spend time and money trying to gain an education and examine how the competition operates. But instead of gaining an upper hand, all they have is knowledge of how the competition did it ten or twenty years ago. Schools are always behind, and if you rely on traditional education alone you'll always be behind, too. Believe that inexperience is an asset, allowing you to think outside the box in ways your competition can't even imagine.

3. **No One Will Take You Seriously** – Believing you're too young to get respect from the business community can be paralyzing, so you wait for the perfect time to start – which never, ever comes. The proof is in the pudding. The earlier you start, the faster you will gain experience, and the faster

you will succeed. Besides, the Internet allows you to act like a big business, even if you're conducting business in your underwear. You're never too young to become an entrepreneur – you don't even need a driver's license to launch your first company!

4. **Your Idea Is Impossible Because it's Never Been Done** – So many people are trapped by the belief that something can't be done just because no one else has done it before. Again, the immediate result is inaction. And the end result is watching someone else achieve your "impossible" idea. Every invention, every business, every great idea had to have a first time. If no one has ever done what you want to do, be excited! You have the advantage, because you will be the first to pull it off.

Do you see how, before you even get started, your limiting beliefs have built a wall so high and so strong your progress from (A) is immediately blocked and pushes you in a new direction? It is impossible to achieve (B).

I call these limiting beliefs "The Wall." The Wall is insurmountable and is more powerful than any physical barrier could ever be. There is no method of knocking it down or destroying it other than to vanquish The Wall by creating a channel of enabling beliefs.

"But wait a minute! If I believe that I need money to start a company, and then I get money that will clearly knock down The Wall, I can destroy The Wall without changing my beliefs."

Not true. Access to money has not knocked down The Wall; it has actually made The Wall bigger and stronger. You have not changed your belief that you can't start a business without money. You actually proved to yourself that you needed money. The Wall of "can't start without money" is made temporarily irrelevant since you have money for now. But the belief is still there, larger than ever. The next time you are in a situation that you believe requires money you don't have, your limiting belief will stop you in your tracks. Navigating around your limiting beliefs doesn't knock The Wall down; it makes it higher.

TPE TIP

Service Sales – Use Elance.com, Guru.com or other freelance websites to quickly land projects that fit your capabilities and desires. This will cost a few bucks, but it is another inexpensive way to get started without putting money into a website.

Envy This

Envy. Until recently, I didn't appreciate how damaging envy was to my own progress. And as my envy of others diminished, my own entrepreneurial progress picked up with even more momentum.

I used to see successful people who clearly were ahead of me, and I would acknowledge their success outwardly. Inside, though, I was telling myself that they were probably unhappy pricks, that they were silver spooned and undeserving of what they had. A million other thoughts would cross my mind, mentally knocking people down well below me, which made me feel good, at least for a while. But the next time I saw a successful person my envy would be even greater, and I would repeat the process.

Then I had an epiphany. When I envy someone, I am just building more limiting beliefs. I am actually increasing the size of The Wall that I am putting in front of my own success. When we envy someone else, what we are saying is that they have achieved something that we should have, but we didn't (and can't), so screw them. They have something that no one deserves, so they can go eat crap. Either way, we are saying we can't have what the other person has. That is a HUGE limiting belief.

Envy of others builds an insurmountable wall to our own success. Instead of envy, truly applaud those people. Aspire to be like them in the aspect that you formerly envied. Thank them for having blazed the path before you and making your path to success much easier. Ask them how they did it, what they did. You may be surprised at how much they help you.

You must confront limiting beliefs head-on and change them. That is the only way to dissolve The Wall. You must convert the beliefs that block new beliefs that help you, beliefs that create The Channel.

The Channel of Enabling Beliefs

To be a successful entrepreneur, you need to train your mind and your heart to have enabling beliefs. Just as when you have an off day and come back harder and stronger the next day, your enabling beliefs have created a path that moves you forward toward your goals, even though things went awry. I call this belief conduit "The Channel."

What if we change our beliefs from the previous example? Let's create the new beliefs set:

1. You have no money, which enables you to focus your inge-
    nuity and your energy to market your product better than
    any competitor.

2. You have never done this before, allowing you to come up
    with outside-the-box, unheard-of ideas that will destroy
    your competition.

3. You are young and professional which commands huge re-
    spect in the business community.

4. No one has discovered a fast-growth method in your indus-
    try, and so your innovative talent will accelerate your growth
    and put you well in front of the pack.

By revising the beliefs that built The Wall, you not only remove the
limitations, you actually create The Channel. Through The Channel
your momentum is pushed forward. Even if you get bumped off
track your enabling beliefs keep you moving forward.

Here are my best tips for creating a channel of enabling beliefs:

Realize Nothing's Impossible – When you say and believe something is impossible, you set up a giant roadblock to success. Today,
if I told you that teleporting is possible, you would laugh at me. If I
told you flight was possible you would say of course it is. Any moron
knows that. But the same statement about flight made in the 1800s
made people laugh and say, "impossible." Right here, right now, stop
saying something is impossible. There is always a way, and you need
to seek it out. I can't wait until the first teleporter is invented so I can
say, "I told ya so!" Nothing is impossible.

Ask Better Questions – We have all heard the statement, "There is no such thing as a stupid question!" Wrong! I am here to tell you there *are* stupid questions, and they are everywhere. People ask me the same lame-ass questions over and over. One of my favorites is, "How do I get an investor to give me money?" As if investors are like Mom and Dad, and they want me to help them come up with a convincing story that will get them a new car, or whatever else they feel entitled to having. Stop asking stupid questions. Ask a better question. Be the first to ask, "How would I SHOW an investor a 200% ASSURED return on her money?" Or, "How could I SHOW an investor how we could both come out as winners?" Better questions get better answers.

Watch Someone Else Doing It – So many times, if we just opened our eyes, we would see that someone is already doing what we thought impossible. We just need to apply it to ourselves. The Wright brothers just needed to look at a bird to see the possibility of flight. Then they asked a great question: "How can we use what we know from a bird to make a contraption that will allow people to fly?" If someone or something else is already doing it, it sure ain't impossible.

Ask How – I once thought photographic memory was something a few weirdos were born with, but was impossible for the common folk such as myself to learn. I even saw a demo in which a guy memorized a detailed list of fifty things in order. I thought he was a freak. Then I asked him how he does it and he actually told me. Man! It was easy once I understood it. I tried it, and holy smokes, now *I* can memorize a useless list of fifty things. I am now the freak. Move over Criss Angel, I am now the mind-freak! Mind-freak!

Do It Yourself – Until you prove something to yourself, you will never believe it. Sometimes the proof is in the puddin'. Challenge yourself and try something that is contrary to your limiting beliefs. Don't try it to prove yourself right; instead, try it with the absolute commitment to prove yourself wrong. When you actually achieve it, you will have achieved a new enabling belief. Being wrong never felt so right!

Take Baby Steps – If you need to make a 180-degree change in your beliefs, you have to start changing one degree at a time. Put the majority of your energy into making the first little change. Once it is accomplished, congratulate yourself for being one degree closer, and then go for the next one. Don't try to tackle everything at once; address it one small baby step at a time. TPEs know their millions are made by grabbing the first $100 and then the next.

View the Glass as Half Full – When faced with any situation, you need to focus on finding only the benefits. In some situations, there may be very few benefits and many, many problems. Focusing on the problems will yield nothing. You need to exploit the benefits that you can find, even if they are few and far between. Even if your glass has only one drop of milk in it, there is still something to drink. Or, if just one sheet hangs from the roll, you can still wipe… you get the picture.

Write and Research – Often, many people say they know something, and when you ask them how they know, they respond, "I just know." It is an easy, lazy way to build The Wall of limiting beliefs. When you have a belief that is preventing strong progress, write it down. Then research the hell out of it. The information you find will often destroy your belief and get you into The Channel of strong momentum.

When It's Over, Move On (The French Toast Incident) – Just because something happened in the past doesn't mean it will happen again. What I'm about to share with you is corny, but embarrassingly true. Until I was eighteen years old, I avoided eating French toast like the plague. I knew that French toast would make me sick because, at the age of six, I ate French toast and got horribly sick minutes later. I threw up for days. I mean, it was a vom-fest. Putting one and one together, I knew that French toast was the culprit. I vowed in that moment never to eat it again.

Then it happened. At age eighteen I was placed in the horrible position of either starving to death or eating the only thing left – French-fucking-toast. With a quivering lip and ten gallons of Aunt Jemima, I dug in. It was delicious. Surprise, no puking! Years later my mother told me that when I was six and puked for days I had the flu. It wasn't the French toast after all. So just because it happened once before doesn't mean it will happen again. Don't let twelve years go by without eating French toast.

When it comes to entrepreneurial success you have to know that it is absolutely, unquestionably, hugely important to defeat or change your limiting beliefs. Only once you have The Channel of enabling beliefs can you even begin to march forward and build your desires.

TPE TIP

More Product/Service Sales – If you don't want to spend a penny, use Craig's List to get the word out. Listing products or services costs you squat.

Getting Past Day One

Knocking down your Wall and building your Channel is big, powerful stuff. But how do you hold fast to your beliefs past that first inspiring day? The truth is, you'll have to work on building your Channel daily in order to make it stick. Here are a few tips to help you maintain your TPE mindset:

Go with Your Gut, Not Your Logic

Your beliefs are your core emotional responses; they are NOT based on logic. In other words, your beliefs are the thoughts behind your thoughts. If you are saying out loud, "I will succeed," but your gut is saying, "You can't, 'cause you suck," your gut will win out, and you will suck. I cannot overemphasize the importance of this. We all achieve what we believe deep down inside – this ain't hocus-pocus, this is the science of how humans operate. Be very mindful of the thoughts behind your thoughts... your gut.

Join the Right Mob

Changing your beliefs doesn't typically happen with a snap of the fingers. But one very effective method for changing your beliefs is to identify the people already achieving what you want and entrench yourself in their group. If you measure the common traits of your five closest acquaintances, you are equal to that. Choose the people you hang out with based upon what you want to be. Absorb everything you can from them and learn at every opportunity. Take them out to dinner, attend network events with them, and just plain ol' spend time with them.

And here's my advice about staying *grounded in your beliefs* as you launch your business:

Share Your Thoughts

You wouldn't believe how many people approach me saying they have the next billion dollar idea, but are afraid to share it with me or anyone else in fear of the idea being stolen. Ultimately, the thoughts fade away, and another inspired moment is lost. Share your ideas with trusted individuals, just don't give away your "secret ingredients" if you can avoid it. Sharing your ideas strengthens your belief in them, and soon you will be acting on that strength to support your ideas.

Know that responses to your ideas are free and often worth about that much. But if you share your thoughts with "been-there done-thats," the collective feedback may be invaluable. As you share your ideas, your beliefs will grow, and people will start holding you accountable. The upward spiral begins.

Ignore or Adore

Don't ignore the naysayers if they are your prospective clients or trusted individuals who have already tried what you plan to do. Do ignore them if they are just trying to stand in your way or are speaking from a vantage point of ignorance. The best feedback is from people who have already done what you are doing.

I can't tell you how many people have told me not to start a business and that entrepreneurialism is assured failure; of course, none of these naysayers has any experience to back up those opinions. When I speak with successful entrepreneurs, their response is the polar opposite. They freely share the paths they have already blazed in launching a company. Always adore the people who have been there and done that; the others are to be ignored.

Grow a Pair

That's right, damn it. At some point every business will have a dark day, month or, God forbid, an entire year. You are going to struggle for a while. Even the big guys struggled. Gary Erickson, the founder of Clif Bar, maker of organic energy and nutrition foods, had to live in a garage, work a day job, and stay up all night making product. Early entrepreneurial success is defined by surviving, not thriving. Set out with the beliefs, focus, and actions to grow rapidly and strongly, knowing that initially it is all about just getting up off the ground.

Seriously, Grow a Pair

The worst thing is to never even try in the first place. Sadly, most people don't. Most people sit on the sidelines and let opportunity after opportunity go by. What a damn shame it would be to have your last words be, "I never even tried." Listen up, Tiger, you may fail and you may suck, but you will only know if you try. Gary didn't give up when his equipment kept breaking down due to the thickness of his Clif Bar mixture. He overcame seemingly insurmountable obstacles to launch what is now one of the most successful and revered American health food companies.

Early entrepreneurial success is often defined by survival. But my bet is that once you get started, you will naturally get your feet under you and not just survive but thrive. So find that footing, start a confident walk, and then run a winning entrepreneurial marathon. Worst case? You don't learn, don't grow, and you fail; don't worry, another Toilet Paper Entrepreneur who *did* succeed will have a job waiting for you. The greatest failure is never to have tried at all. Seriously, grow a pair and go for it.

TPE TIP

Better Affirmations: Standing up and making a statement, or an affirmation, saying, "My business is great," will probably not convince you that it is. And the thought under the thought will be the opposite. Use this trick: Put the words "She thinks" or "He thinks" before your claims. For example, "He thinks my business is great." This affirmation will naturally work, since your mind is configured to make it true. If someone else believes something positive about us, we naturally believe and build in that direction. This is some twisted mind screwing, but it sure as hell works. Give it a try. (This works on picking up members of the opposite sex, too, at least so I am told. I am a happily married man – or, should I say, "My wife thinks I am a happily married man.")

Mission I'm Possible

Many people say something is impossible because it hasn't been done before. I'm gonna get a little Anthony Robbins on you now. If you look at the word impossible, it can actually be split into two words "I'm" and "Possible." From now on, whenever someone says something is impossible, hear the word as, "I'm Possible." As in, I'm possible and will achieve whatever I believe.

Before the Wright brothers, people thought it was impossible to fly, and it was. Then the plane was invented, and now flight is possible.

If the Wright brothers had listened to the people who said it was impossible for humans to fly, we might not have planes today. Progress often involves beating the odds and doing the impossible.

Today we look at flight and know that of course it is possible. It's a no-brainer. The reason you and I believe that is that when we were born, flight already existed; it's all we know. For many people the Internet is the same way. Of course it is possible, it exists, it works, it's great. If you rewind history to before Al Gore invented the Net, the thought of instantaneously exchanging a letter with anyone anywhere in the world was crazy. Today, you are mocked for using postal mail instead of email. Even email is getting stale; it is the new snail-mail. IM-ing is the way to go. All things are impossible things before they exist.

What's impossible today? Seek out people saying something is impossible; they are often venting a frustration. TPEs know that behind every frustration is a new product or service, and behind every impossibility there is a goldmine of business opportunities.

Is it "impossible" to get good food at your college? Is it "impossible" to get through security at the airport? Is it "impossible" to teleport? Is it impossible to _____? Make whatever is "impossible" today your business. Make it possible.

TAKE ACTION NOW!

Before you move on to the next chapter, take half an hour to complete the following three exercises. Otherwise, it's all concept and no application. You need to know your beliefs backwards and forwards — they are the foundation of your success.

1. Expose your Wall. Make a list of all of your limiting beliefs, no matter how silly they sound. If you're stumped, use your list of excuses as a jumping off place.

2. See your Channel. Write down your enabling beliefs, those certainties that help you take chances and ponder greatness. Stumped again? Think about your accomplishments. How did you get there? What did you know for sure that helped you achieve?

3. Knock down your Wall; build up your Channel. This is really just a beginning, because you will continue to uncover both limiting and enabling beliefs as you go through life. For now, debunk those beliefs with affirmative statements, and make a plan to act on your enabling beliefs, new and old.

CHAPTER 3 – THE FIRE IN YOUR BELLY

"Catch a man a fish and you can sell it to him. Teach a man to fish and you ruin a wonderful business opportunity."

- Karl Marx

The foundation to any TPE's success is listening to and following her heart, traveling where it insists she go. Your heart is simply the map to your company's destiny; your head is the navigation system.

When nature sends a rumble through your stomach, you move quickly and deliberately to the bathroom. When you arrive, you spend a few moments preparing for the work at hand. This is your mind navigating the situation.

What is the chance of interruptions? Pretty high? Not good. Does the door lock? Shit! It doesn't! Son-of-a-bitch, the door doesn't even close completely. Time's ticking; gotta move faster, gotta think. How about wedging the magazine rack and some bath towels behind the door to slow down any unexpected guests? You must prevent being caught mid-maneuver. Now, with the door addressed, is there proper ventilation to take care of any "periphery" issues? Most importantly, is there adequate noise to cover up any unexpected music? Maybe it's smart to do a few practice runs clearing your throat, just in case there's a need for cover-up sounds.

All systems checked. Time to get to work. Oh crap! You forgot to check for a roll of TP. Sure enough, a mere three dangling sheets are waving in the breeze. You're caught again with your shorts around your heels. But you're a Toilet Paper Entrepreneur. This one is easy to navigate. Time to start limbering up your leg.

What To Do? What To Do?

Do something that you want to do because you love it, are passionate about it, and because it has a positive impact. Whoopty-doo! Very freakin' noble, right? Doing what you love is a great starting point, but that won't necessarily bring home the bacon. I could spend months talking about high-performance cars because I love them, am passionate about them, and they are exhilarating. But unless I can make a comfortable living at it, it is just an expensive hobby.

Passion is the starting point. There is no question about it. If you aren't passionate about your vocation, you will have a real tough time sustaining a start up, let alone living through the dark days. And if you aren't passionate about what you do, someone else who is passionate about it is going to kick your ass into next Sunday.

Your long-term success requires a growing number of customers, consistent cash flow, and your ability to outmaneuver the competition every step of the way. Before you dive in with your heart, first dive in with your head and make sure you can say a resounding YES to each one of these questions:

1. Can you make significant money doing this? Meaning, is it realistic that this business will bring in enough bacon for

you to cover all your expenses AND stash A LOT away into savings?

2. Can you make money consistently? Meaning, is it realistic that this new venture will yield a regular, predictable, and growing flow of cash into the company?

3. Can this venture be started with little or no money?

4. Do you want this venture to be an entrepreneur instead of a freelancer? If you want to be a freelancer, you are simply an employee without a boss. A freelancer focuses on mastering the craft, while an entrepreneur focuses on building the systems that support the craft.

5. Do you want to consume this product/service desperately, but can't find it? If you do, you ARE the focus group.

6. Do you know people who aren't friends and have the same interests as you? Do they also really want this product/service and they can't find it either?

7. Is this business consistent with your values? For example, frugal types would be better off starting the next Old Navy rather than the next Polo.

8. Are people polarized on your concept? Meaning, do some people think it is a great idea and others think it stinks? Polarizing people is a major key to success because it brings recognition from both sides. The side that hates you talks about it, and the side that loves you defends you. See how polarizing concepts get both sides talking about your business?

9. Is your business a one-shot, make-or-break deal, or can it be flexible and change as it grows? You may not get it perfectly right on the first go and may discover new things about yourself. A little flexibility in the business offering can go a long way.

Building your business on a foundation of passion is clearly the most important part of sustained entrepreneurial success, but passion alone won't make you successful. Backing it up with positive answers to all of these fundamental market-demand questions increases your chances for success tenfold.

With passion and potential on your side, it's time to back them up with conviction, a set of Immutable Laws that form the backbone of your company.

TPE TIP

Business Cards – You don't need them to get started, and when you become a big shot you won't want to hand them out. So skip buying them for now and instead collect other people's cards when you meet them. Send contacts a follow-up email, and let your signature act as a virtual business card with all your contact info and links to your website, blog, or social network pages.

What Do You Stand For?

There is a business, located right outside Sydney, Australia, called Gorgeous Things. Its Founder, Lesley-Ann Trow, struggled for years with her company. While she had always made enough money to live, she never really prospered, and she never really felt energized about her vocation. Entrepreneurialism, for her, was a kind of tunnel that seemed to have no light at the end.

It all changed in a moment when she recognized that her personal values were regularly being compromised, downplayed, or ignored in order to deliver what the customer wanted. Her wow moment came when she conceded that the constant challenge to her values was a result of her own activities and beliefs.

She immediately took action, and her business changed radically. Lesley-Ann identified her own five Immutable Laws that she had always had but never really acknowledged, let alone documented. She wrote down everything she stood for and everything she did not. Then she changed her business.

Everything in the company had to comply with her Immutable Laws or it was removed. If a product was not consistent with her values, even though it was a big seller, it was removed. If a vendor did not share values, even though it was an inexpensive source of product, the relationship ended. She no longer tried to sell products, electing instead to share stories about her Immutable Laws and how her products supported these values.

Business started to increase exponentially. Old products that were consistent with her Immutable Laws started to sell like never before. A redesigned website that spoke entirely to her values now drew over fifty times the amount of traffic it previously had. Consumers sharing the same Immutable Laws came back more frequently and bought more. Most importantly, she is now happy, very happy. In Lesley-Ann's own words, "Having your own company that mirrors your personal value system is just like having a soul mate. I couldn't imagine anything better." Her business is out of the tunnel, and the sun is shining brightly.

Immutable Laws (A Filter for Everything)

I value and believe in go-givers. If someone wants to take, take, take from me, I push them away as fast as you can say, "Blood sucking, life draining bastard." But if someone genuinely is out to help others, to help her common man, I applaud her and want to associate with her. I, too, go out of my way to help others. When someone tries to take advantage of me, watch out, it is totally inconsistent with my beliefs and I will be pissed. I thrive in making, building, and participating in clear win-win situations because that is my internal rule.

We all have our own mix of unique internal rules we abide by. It is these values that we constantly adhere to, deviating from them with rare exception, that I call our Immutable Laws. When we do deviate from them for some reason, our emotions punch us dead center in the face and remind us how bad it is to compromise our own internal laws. Like the long arm of the law, every time we break our own laws our conscience catches us and punishes us. To be successful as an entrepreneur, you must abide by your own Immutable Laws.

Your values say a lot about who you are, which in turn says a lot about the type of business you will create. You must ensure absolute consistency between your values and your business. If everything you do in your company is consistent with your values, you will be happy and always inspired to work.

But Immutable Laws are far more than the sources of your inspiration and emotional satisfaction; they are the filters for every consideration in your business. Who should you hire? What should you sell? How should your customer service function? What vendors should you work with? Who are the customers you want to service? Any question you have about your business must pass through the filter of your Immutable Laws. If they don't match, don't do it.

The Immutable Laws are the spine of your business. If your spine gets out of alignment, your ability to progress will be greatly compromised, and your company will be hunched over, limping along instead of striding forward. If you break your spine, you will be paralyzed, and your company will fail to survive. Your job, TP Entrepreneur, is to be the chiropractor for your business. You must keep your company's spine in perfect alignment by ensuring that every part of the company body is consistent with your Immutable Laws.

Now that you know how absolutely critical they are, it is time to discover your own Immutable Laws. The good news is that you already know them. The bad news is that they still exist at an emotional level and not as conscious thought. To find them, you need to reflect on your past and consider every situation that pissed you off and every situation that made you feel happy. What is the common thread in the situations that upset you? What were the reasons *behind* the reasons you got pissed? Which values were compromised?

Ask similar questions about the situations that have made you happy. What were the common threads in situations where you were happy? What are the real core reasons you were happy? What is it about those situations that naturally made you happy every time? What values of yours were elevated during those situations?

Some common values many entrepreneurs discover and use to set the stages for their companies include:

- Risk-Taking

- Independence

- Honesty

- Leadership

- Teamwork

- Helping

- Security

- Trustworthiness

- Artistic Creativity

This list is good but not nearly good enough. It's BORING! Would you want to work for a company that had sterile values like that? These filters are way too broad, they don't make clear visuals in your head and they are way too lame. If they are not evoking strong visceral emotion in you, you need to dig deeper, much deeper, to find your own Immutable Laws.

Once you define your values, document them in a way that sings with *your* soul. Don't write them to comply with what your mother likes, or what you think customers want to hear, or what your lawyer friend said is most professional. If you water them down, you will only hurt yourself, and over time your emotions will rise up and punch you in the face again. Your Immutable Laws need to raise the hair on the back of your neck every time you read them, every time you speak them and every time you hear them.

TPE TIP

Meeting Rooms – Nothing's better or cheaper for meetings than a nice hotel lobby. Find a few in your area with quiet, comfortable sitting areas and a power outlet to plug in your laptop. Small business incubators often have free or low-cost meeting space for start-up businesses, or you may be able to rent a library meeting room for next to nothing. And if you have an accountant or attorney that you have used, why not ask him for his conference room?

Since you are still reading this book, you are clearly the edgy type and would likely be as bored by the prior values as you are excited by these:

- No Dry Humping – This is a value of Hedgehog Leatherworks, a TPE company that never "dry humps" its customers with spam, sales literature, or cold calls.

- Blood Money – The TPE company Action Figure Woman treats its money as if it were blood, building a constant "blood reserve" so that if there is ever an emergency, it can survive. My company uses this Immutable Law, too, with our own spin.

- Positivity or Death! – A value of my mentor, Howard Hirsch, this Immutable Law is about choosing to work only with people with a positive attitude. Howard once ran a help wanted ad that read, "Experience irrelevant. Positive outlook on life mandatory," and the right candidates with the right values applied for the job. Howard Hirsch, un-equivocally, is a Toilet Paper Entrepreneur.

- Dive on the Grenade – This Immutable Law is about cultivating a company wherein everyone supports each other. When there is a problem, the person closest to it, be it the President or an intern, is expected to jump on the problem and fix it.

- No Dicks Allowed – This is one of my values. Life is too short to deal with people who are curt, rude, or just out for number one. In plain English – life's too short for dicks.

- Just Like Butta – This is a value from Roof Deck Solutions, LLC, a company that installs high-end outdoor patios for apartments in New York City. Every project they are engaged in involves extremely complicated logistics. In order to keep the customers worry-free, the projects must run as smoothly as butter. So, Roof Deck Solutions only works with vendors and only hires employees who thrive under extreme pressure and share in the value of having things run "just like butta."

- Give To Give – Another value of my company, this Immutable Law is about giving for the joy of giving without expecting anything in return. Likewise, we work hard for the joy of working hard. Oddly enough, it all comes back to us anyway.

- Good Enough Ain't Good Enough – Another Hedgehog Leatherworks value stating that every product and customer experience must be great. Not good but great. This Immutable Law hangs on the wall in their St. Louis workshop, reminding everyone that each product must be perfect.

- Turn the Turtles – Matt Kuttler, the President of ReStockIt, articulated this Immutable Law. Anytime a customer is struggling with a problem or question, the team at ReStockIt jumps into action to get things right. Just as with a turtle on its back, a little effort will get the customer on her feet again and moving forward. Matt Kuttler is a Toilet Paper Entrepreneur.

- We DO Know Jack! – Another carryover value from my former company, this Immutable Law is about knowing the customer inside and out. We routinely received tech support calls, and our team was required to know the answer – and the customer, sometimes named "Jack," – extremely well.

Now we're cooking with gas! These Immutable Laws speak to me and awaken a strong curiosity about what they mean. They speak as clearly to what they are as to what they aren't. They absolutely make vivid, clear pictures in my head (don't ask me about the "Dry Humping" one). And they will absolutely resonate with a select few people and be rejected by many. That's what you want.

The most manageable number of Immutable Laws is three to five. While technically you can have tens or hundreds, that many are way too detailed and too hard to remember. Boil them down to your core values, the essence of what you believe.

Once you identify your handful of Immutable Laws, focus on your gut emotional response to those words. When a value has a strong emotional tie to you, it is a critical value and a perfect Immutable Law. If you don't feel it, ditch the law.

"But I want to have values that everyone can understand," you say. Wrong! Watering down your core values is a mistake. Listen, not everyone will share your values, nor should they. The world would be a boring place if they did. Some people do share your values; those are the people whom you want to reach. They will be your best colleagues, your best vendors, and your best customers. Be true to yourself, and the right people and opportunities will filter to you. Consistent application of your Immutable Laws will build a healthy company, and you will be happy. Guaranteed.

The Why Guy Finds His Why

In the fall of 2005, Simon Sinek hit rock bottom. He felt like a failure and was intimidated by everyone he met. Simon craved the feeling of success more than anything else. He didn't know *exactly* what was missing, simply that something was missing.

Simon started to look to the people and companies that inspired him, fascinated by how these companies inspired others. Steve Jobs and Apple. Richard Branson. Martin Luther King, Jr. It was in studying these people and companies that Simon made an amazing discovery. It didn't matter what they did; what mattered was that they knew *why* they did what they did. Simon set out to know unequivocally why he did what he did.

After looking back over his whole life, Simon saw a pattern to his success. He realized that he felt the most successful when he was most inspired and when he inspired those around him. Simon had discovered his calling, his purpose.

Today Simon Sinek is the leading authority for entrepreneurs who seek their purpose, for those who want to discover their Why. His business and his life are far from rock bottom. In fact, he's felt more successful and enjoyed more success every day since he discovered his Why. Simon Sinek is a Toilet Paper Entrepreneur.

Your ideal customers will be attracted to your business because it speaks to them. They share the values of your business; they want what it stands for; they buy the Why. Your company is a reflection of you. Serving your life's purpose ensures the success of your company. As Simon Sinek says, "You must live and serve your Why."

TAKE ACTION NOW!

Part Two is but a page away, but if you don't stop and complete these three exercises now you'll miss out on something crucial. And no, I'm not just saying that.

1.   What do you stand for? What standards do you uphold in your personal life? What do you expect from yourself and others in your life? In what aspects of your life do you waffle a bit? What are the areas where you will not move a muscle? Do you need to loosen up or have more conviction?

2.   Your set of Immutable Laws is the backbone of your company. Building on your own values and ethics, what are the Immutable Laws of your company? How do these Immutable Laws benefit you, your staff, your investors, and your customers?

3.   What's your Why? Why are you an entrepreneur? Why did you choose your specific industry? Why, Why, Why? Keep asking until you get to the heart of the matter.

PART TWO:

The TPE Focus

*"Columbus didn't have a business plan
when he discovered America."*

– Mary Kay Ash

A huge portion of this book is devoted to the entrepreneurial mindset, but quite frankly it's not nearly enough. As Henry Ford said, "If you think you can or can't, you are right." If you are going to succeed as an entrepreneur, you must have enabling beliefs. You must think you can.

From the previous section you should know how nature's calling you, where your passion is, and have an established mindset to ensure you reach your goals. But there is much more to being a Toilet Paper Entrepreneur. Now you must have a maniacal focus. All your attention must be on the job at hand.

When the TP Entrepreneur feels nature's call, that telltale rumble in the stomach, she doesn't waste time devising an elaborate plan, and she definitely doesn't wait it out until the ideal conditions present themselves. Instead, she proceeds with absolute focus. She analyzes the severity of the erupting opportunity and outlines the major actions she needs to take.

For example, she determines how much time she has before she goes into emergency mode. She identifies the nearest clean and quiet "workspace" and checks to make sure it is adequately stocked before getting down to business. The TP Entrepreneur is always ready to manage when challenges come up, as they inevitably do.

Launching and growing a successful business utilizes the same discipline. Elaborate business plans are useless for directing your business. They inevitably become dust-collectors, or, if you're resourceful, toilet paper. Annual goals and five-year projections aren't worth squat, either. What separates the successes from the sloppy disasters all boils down to a few concise, extremely effective plans coupled with decisive action. Which outcome are you gunning for?

CHAPTER 4 – GETTING DOWN TO BUSINESS

"Make everything as simple as possible, but not simpler."

- Albert Einstein

How come we have all heard the phrase, "less is more," yet still behave as if more is more? So many aspiring entrepreneurs believe that the broader the variety of products and services they offer, the more successful they will be. The problem with this is that the more you do, the less effective you are at any one thing. The less likely you are to be exploiting your strengths. The less likely you are to be exceptional. Broad strokes are for ordinary folks.

A tight focus allows you to quickly determine if the path you are following is bearing any fruit or not. Since the path is narrow, when you hit a problem or a roadblock you will catch it right away. With this knowledge, you can adjust speedily and often with few consequences.

Bill Hewlett and David Packard took focus to heart, but only after a few years of initial startup struggle. On January 1, 1939, they kicked off their partnership with a $538 investment and a beat-up drill press. At first, the company was generally unfocused and worked on a variety of electronic and agricultural products.

Hewlett-Packard hit its stride in the early 1940s with spiked market demand for an HP invention called the Model 200A audio oscillator. The invention introduced a level of quality the market had never seen before and was at a price point that couldn't be touched by the competition. And because they focused tightly on the Model 200A, Bill and David were able to determine how to use technology from light bulbs to make and sell a far more reliable product for a quarter of the competitor's price. The result of HP's razor-sharp focus? Possibly the longest-selling simple electronic design in history.

Fast-forward a mere decade and revenues were well into the millions (and that's 1950s money). Hewlett-Packard was a huge success for a couple of guys who used a coin toss to determine the company name. When Dave Packard won the toss, he had the option to select between Hewlett-Packard and Packard-Hewlett. He went with Hewlett-Packard. David Packard and Bill Hewlett are Toilet Paper Entrepreneurs.

Focus Small To Get Big

Name a company that launched to superstardom without a narrow focus. Can't think of one? That's because it's never happened. Look at Microsoft: it skyrocketed to success on DOS, a simple program that made a computer more functional. Today it is a different animal, making software, video game systems, and computer hardware. But when it took off, it was due to its focus on DOS.

Google launched on a search engine. Now look at all the crap it does. Intel did it on processors. Cirque du Soleil did it on circus acrobats. Ford did it on the Model T. Procter & Gamble struggled with candles and then launched when it focused on soap. I challenge you to find any company that grew exponentially by selling a large, varying mix of offerings from the get-go. Only after they saturated the market with their focus did they introduce a mixed offering, but I can't think of one company that launched that way.

Wal-Mart, too, had an absolute focus in its offering. It was lots of stuff, but all at cheap prices. Everything it carried had to be absolutely the cheapest price anywhere or they did not carry it. The lesson here is that your focus does not need to be on one product, per se, but it needs to be on one consistent method of being way different from everyone else.

It seems common sense would dictate that, the more products and services a business can offer to a wider variety of consumers, the more revenue it could generate – the proverbial "one-stop shop." If you can lock a customer into one service, she will likely buy more things from you because she trusts you. The only problem is that the more you do, the harder it is to maintain quality. The old saying goes, "Jack of all trades and master of none." My version goes, "Jackass of all trades OR master of one." Jackass is appropriate, since that's what your customers will think of you when you try to be everything to everyone. No focus and your products, your services, and your customers suffer.

To be a market leader, your company must excel in one laser-beam-focused area. Be better than anyone else, and continue to focus on improvement in that area, or you will be left behind. As you examine your business, can you imagine how less variety in what you offer will result in greater ability to do what you do well? If so, it is time to start doing less. If you can't see your business improving with greater focus, congratulations: you must already be the world leader in your area of expertise.

A word of caution: Avoid burning your foot with a magnifying glass. It f'ing hurts! Focus, like many things in life, is a double-edged sword. When applied appropriately, focus will result in rewards beyond your imagination. Conversely, focusing on the wrong thing will result in a dangerous downward spiral. You are doomed if you focus on the reasons for your problems as opposed to focusing on a resolution. Focus on achieving success and exploiting strengths rather than avoiding problems and resolving weaknesses. Focus on the wrong thing, and you get burned.

TPE TIP

Virtual Meetings – Need to talk and gawk? DimDim.com offers free virtual meeting software. The best part is that you don't need to install it on anything; it runs right off the Net. No untimely computer crashes! Yeah!!!

How To Drive Dangerously Fast, Safely

The power of focus may be best explained through an experience I had driving a powerful car ridiculously fast. For a second, imagine the TV subtitle scrolling by: Do not try this at home. Closed course. Very unprofessional driver…

I had the good fortune of being trained at Skip Barber's racing school, where they taught me how to navigate a hairpin-turn track driving a 550+ horsepower Dodge Viper. Back then they trained people to race those beasts – now they train on lowly 325HP Porsche 911s.

What they taught me at Skip Barber was all about focus. In order to navigate the course at top speeds, I was trained to focus exclusively on the next turn while the car was still piloting the current one. The trainers taught me to focus on where I wanted to go, not where I was, since my peripheral vision was already taking care of that. To go the fastest, I was trained to continually focus on the next turn. Not the current one, nothing beyond the next one, just the next turn.

I also learned what to do should the Viper start spinning out. Again, it was all about focus. I had to focus on where I wanted the car to go and *not* focus on the wall I was trying to avoid. Sure enough, during my first spin I panicked, looked straight at the wall I was heading into, and steered right toward it. But after a few spins and some potentially expensive near-misses, I learned to focus on where I wanted to go. When times were at their worst – meaning a crash was imminent – a successful outcome was achieved solely by my intense focus on where I wanted to be, not on what was currently happening.

The same is true for your business. Narrow your focus on the best products and services you have to offer. Make those few things extraordinary. Focus on and exploit your strengths. Look at where your business is headed, not where it is at this moment. Is your business in a spin? Give your attention to where you want to go, not to what you are trying to avoid. There is no question about it – you get what you focus on, either good or bad. Concentrate on where you want to be, and your chances of successfully getting there are far greater than if you focus on what you are trying to avoid.

The Focus Five

Can you be too narrowly focused? Absolutely! Let's say your passion is in making delicious, fresh pizza and delivering it in fifteen minutes, guaranteed. You could advertise to the entire world if you like, but it would be nearly impossible (remember, nothing's impossible) to launch a business delivering fresh pizza in fifteen minutes to any location in the world.

So what is the right thing to do? Narrow your focus. You could pick an area that you can easily deliver pizza to in fifteen minutes. The problem may be that there are ten competitors in the same area, all with great pizza and loyal customers. Getting a foothold would be difficult.

What if you focused really tightly so as to ensure a market? You could service only the second floor of residents in the Park Avenue Building. With a tight and specific customer base you could quickly enhance your services to cater to these customers, destroying every competitor with a broader market. For instance, you could install a dedicated pizza phone in every apartment on the second floor, or hand deliver a pizza sample every day. You could do a million things that your competition would not have the resources to match. A tighter focus would allow you to overwhelm the competition in service, customer intimacy, and speed.

There is one glaring problem, though. You won't make crap for a living. The focus in our example is way too narrow. While you could out-service other pizza places, you wouldn't have enough prospects to keep business rolling. That is, unless you are selling your pizzas for $10K each. When you focus too narrowly, it becomes difficult to generate a sustainable income.

The Focus Five is a strategy I developed that allows you to focus narrowly enough to dominate a niche, yet broadly enough to make substantial revenue. The goal of The Focus Five is to find the sweet spot for as little direct competition as possible with the greatest market potential. To find the sweet spot, you need to keep narrowing your focus until you have the confidence and research to support an achievement of $5M dollars in annual revenue within five years of being in business with less than five direct competitors.

Use the following equations to evaluate the trade-offs and find the balance in your business focus:

1. NARROWER FOCUS = INCREASED ABILITY TO BE THE BEST

AND

2. NARROWER FOCUS = REDUCED COMPETITION

BUT

3. NARROWER FOCUS = SMALLER CUSTOMER BASE

PLUS

4. NARROWER FOCUS = LOWER POTENTIAL REVENUE

AND ALSO

5. NARROWER FOCUS = SLOWER GROWTH

The idea behind The Focus Five is that you need to be aware of the gains AND losses that a narrow focus provides. Looking at the equations, for example, you'll notice that, as you focus more narrowly, you will increase your ability to be the best and reduce the number of direct competitors. You will also have a smaller customer base, less potential for earning revenue, and, ultimately, your business will grow at a slower pace.

If you can't realistically achieve $5M in the next five years, your focus is way too narrow to grow a scalable business. Without the ability to achieve at least $5M in revenue, you will spend your efforts in the day-to-day operations of your business, doing work and/or servicing customers. What you want is a business that is positioned to scale to the point where you are managing people and constantly improving internal systems – not working to serve customers. You want to build a business that you are continually working on, not in.

The other variable is competition. If there are five or more direct competitors already operating in your niche, you will be in for a serious fight. But if there are only a few competitors (or none), you can gain a foothold much faster.

When you hone in on a niche that is narrow, but not too narrow, and when you use the $5M marker as a goal, you position your business so that it is safe from big players that can, but don't, buy into the market. A company grossing $5M a year is small potatoes compared to the giants of industry. The giants will wait until you have mastered your business and dominated your niche before they make an offer to buy your company. And that, my friends, is a happy, happy day.

Maybe your aspirations are different. You may aspire to make $1M in five years, which will change the formula to succeed. (Hint: it makes it easier.) Or you may have other numbers. The important thing is to find the balance of focus with potential to achieve your goals.

If you are going to err on one side or the other, it is far better to blunder on the side of being too focused. You can always broaden what you do without losing your current customers. The other way around doesn't work so well.

TPE TIP

Word Processing, Spreadsheets, and Presentations – All are free through Google.com. An added bonus is that your documents are accessible from anywhere on the web, and you can collaborate with others. Amazing. Need more flexibility than Google has to offer? Download an entire productivity suite from OpenOffice.com; it's free.

You Gotta Do Better

Conventional wisdom indicates that people are motivated by the desire to increase pleasure and the need to avoid pain. I think that is too complicated. The fact is, everyone is out to feel better, and the sole purpose of your business should be to make the customer feel better. That's it, game over. All the bullcrap aside, feeling better is all that matters.

An entrepreneur launches a business that makes someone else feel better. The Toilet Paper Entrepreneur ensures that he is always better at providing "better" than any of his competitors. Here are some "better" examples:

1. An insurance provider makes its clients feel better because they feel there is a safety net. Ahh, yes, less worries = feels better.

2. A client selects a vendor because she feels he is nicer, more trustworthy, better looking, smarter, more courteous, or any of a million variables. The net effect is that the client feels better working with this vendor, and she selected him based on that feeling.

3. A doctor makes you feel better. At least she is supposed to, and when she doesn't, you are less desirous of maintaining the relationship and vow to go elsewhere. But it is time-consuming to go elsewhere, and that doesn't make you feel better, so you stay with your lousy doctor because that does feel better.

4. We put others down because it puts us up. We feel better, temporarily.

5. A taxman does NOT make you feel better. So you seek out an accountant or H&R Block, and that makes you feel better. Not much better, but better nonetheless. Until you get the bill.

6. A garbage man takes our rotting garbage away. We feel better.

7. You go to a restaurant and order your favorite hamburger. You feel better. They serve it undercooked. Not good. So you consider complaining and asking for a new one. That would make you feel better. But you fear the cook will spit a phlegm bomb dead center on your patty. That would be horrible. So chewing down on raw meat and not saying anything makes you feel better – it's gross, but you avoided confrontation, so you're feelin' fine.

8. Even this stinkin' book was purchased in order to feel better. You will only keep reading if it continues to make you feel better. If the book doesn't make you feel better, you put it down and stop reading. Again, you feel better.

To launch and maintain a successful business, you need to always make your clients feel better than your competitor does. Always.

Your Area of Innovation – Quality, Price, or Convenience

If there can be only one thing, what are you going to be known for? Inevitably, to lead an industry – or even to have a single sale for that matter – you need to be better, faster, or cheaper. You need to have a unique, desirable attribute that no one else offers. This attribute will always be a perceived differentiator of quality, price, or convenience.

Where in your business can you offer quality, convenience, or price that is far better than the competition? Once you find it, pick just one and stick with it for the life of the company. HINT: You must pick the category that fits seamlessly with your beliefs and your Immutable Laws. Then do everything in your power to be the best at it and always, ALWAYS improve on it.

By selecting your key differentiator, you have determined your Area of Innovation – the way to consistently ensure you're the one making your customer feel better. Customers will return to you again and again in search of that feeling.

If you are Wal-Mart, your Area of Innovation is Price. To continue to dominate the industry, Wal-Mart must have an unrelenting focus on providing the best price. If it gets off the Price track, it's in trouble. Could you imagine Wal-Mart offering, for example, a convenient movie rental service that could compete with Blockbuster and Netflix without offering an amazing price advantage? Oh, wait a second; Wal-Mart did do that, and it FAILED MISERABLY. Wal-Mart's movie download service launched in February of 2007, and by December of that same year it was toast, a total failure caused by Wal-Mart's focus on *Convenience* rather than *Price*.

Wal-Mart has grown explosively because it is all about the lowest Price first; everything else, including Quality and Convenience, comes second. Even the mighty Wal-Mart could fail if the company loses focus and compromises Price in an effort to improve another Area of Innovation. Of course, if it increases Quality while first ensuring it leads on Price, it wins.

McDonald's leads on Convenience. The day they start offering burgers that are cooked to order (Quality), they are in trouble, because you will have to wait longer and Convenience will be compromised. But if they can knock out a cooked-to-order burger faster than they prepare their current burgers, then they really have a win. How would you like yours, in five seconds flat?

Mercedes leads on Quality. Can you imagine Mercedes coming out with a competitor to the Toyota Corolla? It would lose, so it doesn't.

Dick's Last Resort restaurant in South Carolina also leads on Quality, but it sure isn't the quality of the food. Instead, it is the Quality of the experience. The waitstaff insult guests, mock their food orders, and force them to wear goofy hats. It's definitely not for people without a good sense of self-deprecating humor. But if you like that type of atmosphere, Dick's is the highest Quality experience you can find anywhere. How many restaurants regularly get five-star ratings on service and atmosphere when their waiters inevitably say, "Is that all you are going to give me as a tip, you cheap bastard?"

The Area of Innovation is where you need to put all of your energy and inventiveness. If your company leads on quality, for example, you need to constantly focus on how to improve quality. Should you ever ignore or compromise quality in an effort to save money or reduce price point or make things more convenient or for any reason, you're screwed. The consumer, who has been buying on quality, will notice to immediately, feel compromised, and typically leave or start the search for an alternative.

Encyclopedia Britannica had a miserable collapse, particularly since it was a beloved American icon. Believe it or not, those giant books were once considered a convenient way to find information. Britannica's Area of Innovation was Convenience, even going so far as to sell door-to-door and deliver right to your living room. But when the customers could benefit from improved Convenience by getting their encyclopedias on CDRom, Britannica just kept printing books.

Britannica failed to stay true to, and continually raise the bar in, its Area of Innovation. The company was quickly surpassed by Microsoft's Encarta CDRom, which was later made obsolete by Wikipedia, all in the name of the same Area of Innovation: Convenience. Wikipedia raised the bar so high on Convenience (instantaneous and unlimited information) that Encarta didn't have a chance. It also raised the bar ridiculously high on Price (free) and Quality (it is a living file and constantly updates and improves). I can't wait to see who kicks Wiki's ass. And trust me, someone will. Maybe it will be you.

What is your Area of Innovation? Is it in keeping with your Immutable Laws, your internal rules? Does it ring true?

Commit to leading in Quality, Price, *or* Convenience, and make sure you pick just one to focus your attention on. Stay in the ballpark with the other two areas, but never, ever, compromise your Area of Innovation in an effort to excel in all three. When you diligently and consistently work to raise the bar in your Area of Innovation, effectively competing with yourself, you stay out of your competition's reach.

Who's Your Ideal Customer?

You are deep into the book now, and this is the first time that we are going to start really digging into identifying your customer. Traditional business training and common logic say that this is your starting point of launching a company. They couldn't be more dead wrong. Starting a company is all about serving your needs, your beliefs, and your values first. By this point you should have a strong knowledge of yourself and a clear vision for what you want. (That is, if you followed the action steps at the end of each chapter!) You are now ready to identify your ideal customer.

Market demographics, trend analyses, and other statistical measures are important, but they only scratch the surface. They surely don't position you to launch successfully. As with everything else in business, you need to start by knowing your destination first. In this case, you need to define your customer so well that you can pick him or her out of a crowded room of thousands of people.

Paul Scheiter can pick a perfect customer out of a crowd in seconds flat. The founder of Hedgehog Leatherworks, the leading provider of leather survival products (talk about a tight niche!), Paul defined his ideal customer early on in his business and experienced phenomenal growth just by *knowing his customers like the back of his hand.*

After launching his company from his college dorm room, Paul soon realized that his sporadic sales were coming from a wide mix of customers. Some were in the military, some were hunters, others were survivalists, a few were collectors, and still more were totally undefined. Paul knew he couldn't possibly cater to so many different types of customers, so he compiled a list of one hundred adjectives and descriptive phrases that defined his perfect customer. He identified his customers' values – specifically those he held in common with them – as well as how they looked, acted, and reacted. Paul even knew his customers' favorite movies.

With these details documented, Paul simply kept his eyes open, and whenever he noticed someone that fit his description of an ideal Hedgehog Leatherworks customer, he struck up a dialogue with them. Sure enough, knowing exactly what he was looking for, Paul quickly met many people with similar interests and values, a few of whom were very influential people within his niche. These people became his friends, made introductions, and brought in more people with similar interests and values.

Paul's business took off and has grown explosively ever since. Within two years of his launch, Hedgehog Leatherworks is recognized as the world leader in high-end performance leather sheaths. Paul has a loyal customer base that floods him with unsolicited testimonials and thank-you notes. Handling all of his testimonials has actually become a challenge for Paul. Now that's a problem to aspire to, wouldn't you say? Paul Scheiter is a Toilet Paper Entrepreneur.

You, too, need to know your customer with this level of detail because, simply put, it makes it much easier to locate, market to, and then sell to them. Consider the tickler questions below when defining your ideal customer. The goal here is to start broad, and then systematically funnel down to the exact customer who will most appreciate, connect with, and benefit from what you plan to offer. Trust me, your ideal customer will share in your Immutable Laws, tremendously value your Area of Innovation, and be a raving fan of your product or service.

This list of questions is far from complete and is simply a starting point. You need to ask an exhaustive series of questions. You will have completed the task of identifying an ideal customer when you are able to walk through a crowd and identify him by the way he looks, behaves, talks, smells, etc. If everyone in a crowd is your potential customer you are way too broad. But if one out of one thousand is clearly an ideal customer, you may have found your perfect niche.

- Where do they live and why?

- What do they cherish? Why?

- What do they hate? Why?

- What is their favorite TV show? Why?

- Do they even watch TV? Why not?

- What would they not be caught dead doing?

- What is the most important part of their daily routine?

- Do they own a car, and if so, what is the make and model? If they own a car, how aggressively do they drive it?

- What pisses them off over and over again about your industry?

- Are they married or single? Are they gay or straight?

- How old are they? How old do they look? How old do they *act*?

Know your prospects better than any of your competitors and you will have an easier time finding them. When they become customers, you will be able to relate to them better. They will come to you easily and stay happily.

As a final thought, recognize that by knowing one group so well, you will not know other groups at all. You may actually upset some people. This is OK. It is actually desirable. You want to polarize people. You want clients who love you and others who don't. If you get the love/hate reaction, you know you are on to something, since your focus is causing exclusion and discomfort with some. Better yet, the people who love you now will have a reason to defend you, further entrenching their adoration because you share a common "enemy." Serve a narrow niche and facilitate growth by exclusion!

You Are Really, Really Good at Very, Very Little

Many entrepreneurs get in the habit of saying, "I can do it" to everyone and everything. I call this the "I Can" syndrome. While it is true you can do many things, you suck at most of them. All of us are naturally talented at only a few things and are mediocre or bad at everything else. Entrepreneurial mastery requires that you learn what your strengths are (few as they may be) and exploit them to the fullest. All the other areas, where you are not strong, need to be handled by other people who *are* super-talented in those areas.

I recognize that this is easier said than done. During the early stages of launching your company, you do, in fact, need to do everything. In addition to stretching every penny you have, you also need to learn the requirements of your business. Over time, as you start to generate cash flow, you need to introduce other experts. As you can afford it, bring on extraordinary staff and/or services that can replace you in the areas that consume a majority of your time and where your talents are weakest. For example, if you have poor attention to detail, which most entrepreneurs do, you will probably want to hire an excellent part-time bookkeeper. Maybe contract with a personal assistant service to help with scheduling and small tasks.

Discover the areas where you are naturally talented. This requires stepping away from the moment and looking at your abilities and experience objectively. Consider your answers to these questions to discover your strengths:

1. What do you do that you look forward to? If you consistently enjoy doing something, it may be one of your strengths.

2. What activity do you push off to do last? When you routinely avoid a certain task, there's a good chance it may be one of your weaknesses.

TPE TIP

Conference Calls – Check out FreeConferenceCall.com for free calls for up to ninety-six people at a time. You can't beat that.

3. In what area do you pick up knowledge very easily? If you catch on to something quickly, it's probably one of your strengths.

4. In what areas do you struggle? These are almost definitely weaknesses.

5. What activities give you satisfaction, a sense of worth, and just make you feel good? These are probably strengths.

6. When a mere three sheets are dangling, what is your instinctive approach? Do you joke your way out, do you work with atypical resources, do you scream for help, do you dive into the shower, or do you say, "Screw it" and just stand up and walk out? The way you handle crises is also one of your strengths.

In every situation in life our *natural* tendency is to lean toward our strengths. But this is typically at a subconscious level. Often we let our logic redirect our course, and do what is not natural. We actually hamper ourselves by trying to improve our weaknesses because our mind is telling us this is what we must do. Listen to your internal guidance, your emotions; if it feels good, if it feels natural, if it feels right, it almost definitely is. Your emotions consistently point you toward your strengths. Build on them.

Know that you have a "super strength" that no one else will ever match: You care more about your business than anyone else. Your company is your baby – your mission and your passion. For some of your colleagues it may just be a job. They may admire and respect you, but at the end of the day it may still just be a job. You alone have the responsibility of ensuring everyone and everything are well cared for and moving forward.

TAKE ACTION NOW!

These next action steps are huge. Unbelievably huge. Huge and crucial to your success. You may even need some extra time to complete them, and your answers may change as you discover more about yourself and your business. Just dig in and see what you can get done in half an hour. If you've got more time, by all means, work it out.

1. Flip back to the section on The Focus Five and read it again. Figure out your Focus Five, working the equation until you come up with a niche you can dominate but in which you still earn at least $5M annually after no more than five years in business. Do not skip this step!

2. Building on your Immutable Laws, choose one Area of Innovation. Consider all of the options before you commit.

3. How well do you know your ideal customer? Write a list of characteristics that describe your ideal customer in detail, right down to his or her underwear. Go with your gut and try not to judge your list. You might be surprised at how many attributes you can come up with right off the bat.

CHAPTER 5 – IT'S ALL ABOUT REGULARITY

"Winning is not a sometime thing. You don't win once in a while, you don't do things right once in a while, you do them right all the time. Winning is a habit. Unfortunately, so is losing."

– Vincent Lombardi

How many times have you heard about the importance of a detailed business plan? Make sure you have ten years of financials. Make sure you can make $100M dollars capturing only 0.1% of the potential market. Make sure you have a strong management team with a strong track record. Make sure you can show clearly where your customers will be coming from and why. Everyone tries to tell you that you need a winning business plan if you ever hope to go anywhere with your business. Well, I'm here to tell you that a business plan is a total waste of time.

Almost every business plan I have ever seen includes excruciating, eye-bleeding detail, discusses irrelevant experience, and is supported by a fantasy "management dream team" willing to work without pay for six months. But that's understandable, because within six months the hypothetical projections show that everyone will be making million-dollar salaries. Yeah, right.

Once a company is up and running, the business plan rarely, if ever, receives a second glance – let alone an update. Instead, it ends up collecting dust on the shelf. What a waste! All of that time, effort, and money spent developing a work of fiction that winds up in the recycling bin. Even if you choose to squander your money on business planning software in an effort to streamline the process, you'll still end up with a totally useless document.

Three documents will launch your business faster and better than any business plan. With these powerful documents, your growth will be limited only by your beliefs and focus. Trash your business plan right now, because I'm about to teach you the power of three sheets (documents): Your Prosperity Plan, Quarterly Plan, and Daily Metrics.

Don't believe you can plan a successful business using just three documents? Read the Declaration of Independence, a one-page document that launched a powerful, free nation and inspired the entire world.

TPE TIP

Accounting System – Intuit's QuickBooks Simple Start offers a free, basic accounting system. When you go big time it is easy (but not free) to upgrade to the professional version. For more free accounting software, try GnuCash.

A Junk Man's $1B Prosperity Plan

Junk isn't the most glamorous business in the world. Would you believe that in the summer of 1998, some guy was daydreaming about how he could change the world by being a junk man? Well it's true, and his name is Brian Scudamore of 1-800-GOT-JUNK? based out of Vancouver, BC.

The idea came to him while fishing one summer day. As thoughts of his life drifted through his mind, Brian reviewed his past ten years of entrepreneurialism. He had built a small rubbish removal business in the past decade, and it was generating a respectable but small $1M plus in annual revenues. Respectable, but not satisfying. That's when it hit him.

Brian dropped his pole and began writing down his expectations of himself and his company. Not mere wishes or hopeful thoughts, but a real vision of his future. He started writing a "Painted Picture," as he came to name it, describing what the future of his company would be like. The document contained grand statements, "unrealistic" goals, and unheard-of expectations. But the document was extremely real to Brian. Every time he read the document, his heart beat faster and his emotions soared. He kept on improving it and improving it. Within a day he had prepared a document that was so compelling to him, so true to his hardwired purpose in life, he just knew this had to become his reality.

Like the Declaration of Independence, Brian's document contained ideal statements that rang true with him. He made commitments that were outrageous to others, just like the small group of men that declared the rag-tag United States army would defeat the military juggernaut of England.

When Brian returned from his weekend trip to the cabin, he had his "Painted Picture," his Prosperity Plan, in hand. He set to action immediately, and slowly but surely hired only those few people who believed in the same vision; the nonbelievers went their own way.

Fast-forward five years. Brian's company, 1-800-GOT-JUNK?, went from $1M in annual revenue to $100M in annual revenue. That is not a typo; $100M in revenue. His newest tweak to his Prosperity

Plan has him doing $1B in annual revenue by 2014. I have a good feeling it's gonna happen. He absolutely believes it is. Brian Scudamore is a Toilet Paper Entrepreneur.

Create a Prosperity Plan

A Prosperity Plan is the overarching, never-changing (but often tweaked) document that describes what your company is all about. It is your written commitment to your company goals and the standards you will abide by to achieve them.

The Prosperity Plan replaces the most powerful part of a business plan, the section that often gets ignored; it establishes the foundation of beliefs for your company and generates excitement. But business plans get shelved and then forgotten. Because your Prosperity Plan is accessible to you at all times, it reenergizes you. It affirms your beliefs. It realigns you with your vision.

Writing a Prosperity Plan is the very first step in starting your company. Creating this document comes before you legally form and register your business, even before you name your company. Your Prosperity Plan details your vision for your company. It defines everything you and your business are about, everything you and your business stand for. How can you have a good company name, a strong marketing message, or accomplish anything with consistency without knowing where you are headed? You can't. That's why the Prosperity Plan is the first order of business.

The formation of your company is all about you. This is so important to understand! It is so different from what we are taught that I need to say this again. Your company is first, foremost, and exclusively

ALL ABOUT YOU. Your customers are critical, but they are second to your wants, because if you're not happy, they won't be either. Your company depends on effective colleagues, but they won't perform well if you are a miserable SOB. The Prosperity Plan must be all about you and what you envision to be the best, happiest, most perfect scenario for YOU.

The Prosperity Plan must be visceral. It must touch you at an emotional level, but it doesn't need to touch outsiders at an emotional level. The Prosperity Plan for my company is powerful; it speaks to my emotions, and I believe in it emphatically. When you read it you may feel that it is lame. You might not be moved by it. It might not even make sense to you. That's cool, because you are you. What matters most is how I feel about my Plan and that I believe in it to my core. Now of course, if you read the document and also believe in it, I want to speak with you. We might make great colleagues.

The Prosperity Plan is also your statement to the world about your beliefs and how you plan to stay true to them. Some people will reject it, most people will disregard it, but some will be drawn to it. The people who are drawn to your Plan are the clients, colleagues, investors, and vendors with which you will be able to build great things.

Here are the key elements of a visceral, motivating Prosperity Plan:

Life Mission – What is your life's purpose? Not your company mission, but your LIFE mission. One informs the other, so as we discussed in Part One, figure out what your heart screams for you to do first. Then figure out how that mission can be played out in a profitable business. If you relentlessly commit to doing what you love, your business will be a force to be reckoned with.

As you discover your life's mission you will probably find your tag line, the short phrase that defines your purpose. Your company name may come to you then, too. The key to discovering these components is that they must always resonate strongly with you; don't worry about anyone or anything else at this phase.

Defining your Life Mission is not an easy exercise. Actually, most of us go through life never discovering it, let alone thinking about it.

Here is how you do it. First, you must believe you have a Life Mission (albeit you may have a different name for it) and that you will discover it. Second, you need to seek it out. Some effective actions you can take:

1. Think about and document your life from the day you were born until today. What were your happiest moments? Why? Would you like to have those feelings and experiences again?

2. Write a list of adjectives that you would like people to use when describing you.

3. Ask your friends to tell you one thing you are absolutely the best at.

4. Write your own eulogy. What stamp would you like to leave on the world?

5. Put a picture of yourself on the cover of your favorite magazine. What magazine is it? Why? What is the title placed above you on the cover? Why?

6. If you could be a guest or host of any TV show in the world, which one would it be? Why? What would you talk about?

7. Who are the ten people you admire most? Why?

8. Write a list of 100 things that you enjoy doing or would like to incorporate into your life.

9. What upsets you the most about the world? Do you have ideas about how to make it better? How would you feel if you were doing that?

10. What have you always wanted to do or experience?

Destiny – Once you know your life's mission, you need to identify your Destiny. This is the "Painted Picture" that Brian Scudamore wrote on that day he was fishing, or the vision document that many business minds talk about. The name you give it is irrelevant. The fact that you have a crystal-clear image of what your company will be is the critical part. Pick a date in the future when you see your company achieving its most notable successes. In my case, I picked ten years out from the day I wrote it.

Think of your Destiny as your ultimate goals and those of your company. Very often they are linked. Write them in as much detail as possible, including how your life will be different when you reach your Destiny. How will you know you've arrived at your goals? How will you measure your success? Will it be in terms of revenue or brand recognition or market domination or something else entirely?

Your Destiny MUST be absolutely 100% believable to YOU. If you write lofty ideas, unrealistic claims, and unachievable targets in your

Destiny, you WILL still achieve them if you truly believe them to your inner core. But if you write lofty ideas, unrealistic claims, and unachievable targets and believe them to be lofty, unrealistic, and unachievable, you don't have a chance. Go back to the drawing board and redo your Destiny *until* you believe it to your inner core. Don't worry about how you are going to get there; I will show you the method in a moment. Simply ensure that the thought behind the thought believes it's possible, or better yet, probable. It must be hitting at your emotional core. You've got to feel it. It must be visceral.

TPE TIP

E-Commerce – Tie your business into PayPal. The system is simple and it works, but they do charge a small percentage for transactions. If you want to go the free route, check out Zen Cart. It works, but it's more complex than PayPal and not as recognizable.

Area of Innovation – As we discussed in the previous chapter, your company can lead in only one Area of Innovation: Quality, Price, or Convenience. Pick the category that intrinsically feels right. Then dig deep into that category and define exactly how you are going to be remarkably different than the competition. What is the area where you just can't be touched? What specifically do customers rave about when they talk about you? This is your Area of Innovation, and you must commit to leading in this area for the life of your business.

If you're just launching your business, choose an Area of Innovation that plays to your strengths. For example, if you've got a fantastic product idea that will surpass the competition by leaps and bounds, you might choose Quality as your Area of Innovation. Or if you know you have the negotiating skills to keep costs down, you might choose Price as your Area of Innovation.

Immutable Laws – You have certain hardwired beliefs that can't, won't, and shouldn't be changed. These beliefs are something we are all born with, and they continue to intensify over time. Not all of us share the same beliefs, and some of us have polar opposite beliefs. When recording the Immutable Laws for your company, they must be YOUR personal values, not a watered down version of what you think others will want to hear.

For example, I believe that in order to get the best out of people I must first give them *my* best. I always say that commitment begets commitment. Loyalty begets loyalty. And I believe it. Occasionally I have been burned, but the vast majority of the time I have not. That's why my values include "Give To Give" and "No Dicks Allowed!"

I have friends who believe someone must show them loyalty first in order for them to reciprocate. Only when they have seen ferocious loyalty do they give the same in return. They have been burned in the past with this philosophy, but the vast majority of times they have not. Their values include "You Gotta Earn It!" and "Prove It."

So who's right? Both! And it doesn't matter. All that matters is that you truly believe your own Immutable Laws and that they are truly consistent with your nature.

Look back on your life, ask friends, and do the exercises outlined in finding your Life Mission. Find your values. I guarantee you have been exercising them all your life already. Document your Immutable Laws as the rules your company will always abide by, no matter what, every time and at every moment.

Remember, this is not about "should," this is about what is meaningful to you. So even if people are telling you that your Immutable Laws are impossible to adhere to or silly or useless, hang tight. When things get hairy or business booms or both, you'll realize how important those Laws are. Immutable Laws will keep you on track; you can draw strength from them in times of crisis and use them to help you make decisions fast.

Community – Finally, at this stage we start talking about someone else besides you! Well, not really. The community is the people you are serving. You will be delivering something to them that is 100% consistent with YOUR Life Mission, is 100% moving YOU toward YOUR Destiny, is extraordinary because of YOUR Area of Innovation, and is consistent with YOUR values. Well, shit, who better to consume this thing than you and people just like you and people who want to be like you? Exactly!

Hands down, you are most capable of connecting with people who share the same values as you and/or aspire to be like you and/or aspire to be somewhat like you. Now that you know all about you and your wants, what people make up the community that has the wants and needs you can satisfy? These are the people you need to speak to, sell to, and service.

Remember, your Prosperity Plan does not have to be realistic by today's standards. In fact, it absolutely should NOT be realistic according to what we know to be true today. Nobody believed a man would walk on the moon; it seemed impossible, the stuff of science fiction or fairy tales. And yet a man did walk on the moon. So think and dream big, and don't let concerns about how you will pull it off influence your Prosperity Plan.

Now go write your own Prosperity Plan. Share it with as many people as possible so that you are forced into accountability. Keep it close by and review it every week. While you may constantly tweak it, the intent of the Prosperity Plan will never change. Check out the Toilet Paper Entrepreneur website (www.ToiletPaperEntrepreneur. com) to download a copy of my Prosperity Plan, which you can use as a template to create your own.

Here's one final tip about your Prosperity Plan: you know you've got it when reading it makes you cry. Yes, you. Your life's mission, your Destiny, all of it should make you blubber like a baby. I don't care how badass you are, discovering your authentic passion is an emotional experience. You have NOT completed this exercise until you break down and cry. I'm not kidding. I got a little choked up there.

Always Be Tacking

The first time I went sailing I was taught a lesson that was so important and applied so much to business that I jumped off the boat, swam ashore, and started writing it down. The boat floated away into the rocks. I had to pay a lot to repair that boat, so you better freakin' learn from this, too!

When sailing a boat, a sailor needs to know where he is in relation to his destination. He has to know which way the wind is blowing and know that it will occasionally change. Finally, he has to periodically look for obstacles that lay in his path, like other boats, landmasses, the Loch Ness Monster, and such.

With these few bits of crucial information, he uses a technique called tacking to navigate as quickly as possible to his destination. He knows that he will not follow a straight line; the changing winds alone will not allow for that. Instead, he will travel in a zigzag-like pattern.

By tacking, the sailor travels a short distance, maximizing the winds and avoiding hazards. He then analyzes where he is in relationship to his destination, adjusts the sails, redirects the boat and continues the zag part of his travels. After another short distance he again evaluates his relationship to the destination and adjusts. Through a regular reevaluation of his current location and the constant destination, he routinely adjusts his actions to redirect the boat toward the destination. The sailor knows that he won't travel a direct line, but by tacking he will promptly arrive at his destination regardless of the way the winds blow and regardless of the obstacles in front of him.

You will make the greatest progress in your business by tacking. The best tacking method for business is using a Quarterly Plan, which I will explain shortly. For now, just know that tacking is essential. Pay attention and navigate only in short segments, readjusting to the final destination only periodically. Don't make me waste all that boat-repair money for nothing.

TPE TIP

Networking Groups – Instead of paying to join a local networking group or traveling to networking events, consider doing it online. Forums are a great starting point. Also consider participating in blogs or starting your own. If you want to do the hybrid of virtual reality meets good ol' fashioned networking, check out Meetup.com and LinkedIn.com. Be a consistent presence and source of participation; these are the folks that stand out and get the business.

Quarterly Tacking

With your Prosperity Plan in the can, you now have a big red **X** showing where you are on the map that is your company's journey, and you know exactly where you need to go and the guidelines you will adhere to in your travels. It's time to put your budding enterprise out on the big, blue ocean and sail toward your destination. As your company travels the rough seas of commerce, the winds will change, obstacles will appear, and you will run into enemy ships. The strategy is to navigate the waters safely while making swift progress to your destination. The strategy to use is tacking.

By tacking your business, your intention is to travel only a short distance as best as you can in the direction of the goal. The Quarterly Plan is a one-page, detailed description of what your business must accomplish in the next ninety days to cover the most ground toward its Destiny. It documents the three most important, overarching goals that must be accomplished in the next quarter. You do know what a quarter is, right? If not, look it up.

The art of proper tacking is to harmonize both speed and distance. Traveling at warp speed in the opposite direction of your destination is of no value; neither is pointing your ship dead on target but standing still. You need to consider every goal carefully and employ a balance of distance, speed, and direction.

Here's the breakdown of the Quarterly Plan process:

1. Even if you are well into the current quarter, write a Quarterly Plan to see you to the end of the quarter.

2. Two to three weeks before the quarter end, commit your full efforts to tie up any loose ends and ensure the completion of the current Quarterly Plan.

3. With this quarter's goals complete, review your Prosperity Plan in detail to see where you are in regards to your Destiny.

4. Only after you have confirmed where you are at this moment and reviewed your destination do you write the plan for next quarter.

5. Complete this process a few weeks before the start of the next quarter. Repeat the process every quarter. Congratulations! You are tacking your business.

The elements of a Quarterly Plan are simple yet powerful. The ideal is to commit to the two or three biggest goals that you can realistically complete this quarter that will significantly advance you toward your Prosperity Plan's Destiny.

Here are the components of The Quarterly Plan:

1. **Overarching Goal** – Write down Overarching Goals for the quarter. These are the overall goals you intend to complete before the end of the quarter, those that get you closer to your Destiny. The goals are not tasks; throughout the quarter there will be many tasks related to the accomplishment of Overarching Goals. Generally, you will have three Overarching Goals every quarter, such as revenue increases, reorganization, or improved employee morale.

2. **Overarching Goal Description** – Clarify your goals by describing each one using a few sentences. Again, this is not a list of tasks; it is simply a full description of what needs to be accomplished in the next ninety days. Any colleague at your office must be able to read the description and know exactly what needs to be accomplished.

3. **Tasks** – Jot down a sequential list of the macro tasks that need to be accomplished in order to achieve each specific Overarching Goal. Each task must be specific enough so that there is a clear and measurable expectation, yet leave room for the person executing the task to exploit his or her own strengths in accomplishing it. I strongly recommend using S.M.A.R.T. tasks – tasks that are Specific, Measurable, Attainable, Responsible, and Time-specific.

   S = Specific: The goal must have enough detail so that it be can be achieved with confidence. A specific goal defines the Who, What, Where, When, and Why.

M = Measurable: The goal must have specific criteria for measuring progress toward achieving the goal.

A = Attainable: The goal must be realistic. If you don't believe it's possible, you won't achieve it. Remember, hard work IS realistic.

R = Responsible: Define ways to stay on track with completing the goal.

T = Time: The goal must have a completion date and time. Without a time frame, there is no sense of urgency, no motivation to accomplish it, because the goal will always be within your time parameters.

4. **Target** – Set realistic target completion dates for each task and then ensure that they are completed in a timely fashion. Highlight the tasks that have been completed in green, and review your progress weekly.

5. **Lead** – Designate a lead person accountable for completing the task. Note two things: first, there can only be one person accountable. If you make several people accountable it will simply result in finger-pointing and he said/she said. Second, this is the person accountable, not necessarily responsible. There is a major difference. Accountable means the person at the end where the "buck stops." The lead may elect to delegate responsibilities in part or in whole to others, but when the shit hits the fan it's his or her problem, exclusively.

That's it! Develop a Quarterly Plan for your top three goals for this quarter, review it, monitor it, and follow it constantly. When the quarter ends, these goals will be accomplished, and it is on to the next, tacking your way to your Destiny.

Download a template copy of the Quarterly Plan from the Resources section on The Toilet Paper Entrepreneur's website (www.Toilet PaperEntrepreneur.com).

Obsidian Launch's Quarterly Plan

Q2 2008

Goal #1 – Maximize Current Partners' Success		
Key Tasks	Target	Lead
1. Forum/Training Meetings – First meeting to occur during Q2. Will schedule monthly	04/04/08	DW
2. Collection of Ideas/Suggestions for each one of our Partners (ideas, leads, suggestions, magazine cut outs, etc.)	04/11/08	MS
3. Viral Marketing – Have 3 templated approaches for viral marketing (Blog, Video, Web)	05/30/08	MJM
4. Key Introductions – Establish method for collecting and making key introductions – including ideal customer parameters, regular communications to Partners, etc.	05/30/08	MJM

Goal #2 – Effective, Regular Obsidian Communication		
Key Tasks	Target	Lead
1. Internal Whiteboard – Create a system for easily sharing internal communications, metrics, etc.	04/30/08	MS
2. Huddles – Enforce daily huddle and have firm agenda with metrics being reported.	04/30/08	MJM
3. Letter from Mike – Have a scheduled monthly internal newsletter going out to partners and employees	06/30/08	MJM
4. Partner Visual Metrics – Have a visual metric board or system for clearly displaying daily goals	05/15/08	PZ

Goal #3 – The Obsidian Way		
Key Tasks	Target	Lead
1. Define Critical Moments and Thresholds – Tracking system and action items for when Partners achieve certain thresholds	05/30/08	PZ
2. Develop Methods to Monitor Threshold – Tracking system that automates the process of tracking Partner progress and notifies Obsidian team/Partners for appropriate actions	06/30/08	PZ
3. Develop Standard Language – Establish and publish consistent use of terms for the	06/30/08	MJM
4. Service Menu – Have a menu that lists all the services we offer our Partners and when we "introduce" the service offering to our Partners	04/30/08	MJM

Your Quarterly Plan is something that you need to share with your entire company, but unlike the Prosperity Plan, this stays confidential to your company and is not distributed. There is no need to give your competitors the details of what you are up to. Hang a copy of the Quarterly Plan over every person's desk. As tasks on the plan get completed on time, highlight them green. If they don't get completed, highlight them red. If they get completed late, highlight them yellow. I mean this literally; have everyone in your office highlight the task on his or her copy of the Quarterly Plan.

How important is this? Critical! Everyone in your entire company will know exactly what is going on with the Quarterly Plan, and since they are the ones marking it up, they are involved even if they are not directly involved. No one wants to see red, either, so your team will all be pushing to keep it green!

As an added bonus, the highlighting becomes a very simple and quick way to measure your progress. If you have all greens, you are cruising along and may want to set more aggressive goals in the future. Mostly green with a few yellows is great – you got everything done and hopefully pushed to make huge strides. Reds are a no-no. Either you are setting unrealistic goals or you are not committed to your plan. When you see red, you sure as heck better get the roadblocks and problems corrected for next quarter.

And remember to celebrate when you've achieved your goals for the quarter. Rewards do not have to be expensive or even have any monetary value. Praise and acknowledgment are always welcome and always free. A nice lunch on you ain't a bad idea either.

Every Day, Review Your Metrics

Now that you know where your destination is, and you have your vessel tacking to it, you need to monitor the ongoing conditions. What if you have a tear in a sail, or a big wave damages your boat and that starts filling with water? You need to regularly inspect and/or have your crew report on the conditions of the ship. No one promised it would be smooth sailing!

Daily Metrics are the final component that replaces the lame, traditional business plan. Daily Metrics are the handful of numbers that instantly identify the health of the company, day in and day out. Is cash flow tight? The Daily Metrics can identify that. Are sales trends

TPE TIP

Computers – I am sure you didn't spend as much time at the library as you should have during college, so take this as an opportunity to catch up. Many libraries will give you free, unlimited access to computers with high-speed Internet connectivity. Need more computer time? Look into college campuses, cybercafes, and friends who will lend you their offices after hours. And if you are a hot-shot and have your own laptop already, you can hop on the free Internet access many of these places provide. Just do us all a favor and stay off the porn, will ya?

strong? The Daily Metrics can identify that. Is internal productivity dropping significantly? The Daily Metrics can identify that, too.

Building on your Prosperity Plan and your Quarterly Plan, identify the three to five most critical numbers you can review, every day, to ensure you are progressing properly. Each Daily Metric must be a single number and/or gauge and must clearly identify progress toward your Prosperity Plan and Quarterly Plan. The metric, if appropriate, can have a plus or minus associated with it to identify if it is an improvement or deterioration from the previous day.

For example, all of our clients have a Daily Metric we call the "Cash Capacity." We get the number by taking our total current cash on hand and dividing it by accounts payable and payroll for the next sixty days. We know that if the number ever drops below 1, we are in a weak cash position. When our Cash Capacity number is between 1 and 3, we are in a healthy position. If our Cash Capacity number goes above 3, then we are in a bloated position, and we put the money into interest-bearing accounts or make capital investments. Every day this number and other Daily Metrics are communicated to our entire company. Every day.

The goal of Daily Metrics is to know your current status as well as to anticipate how future prospects look. For example, a fuel gauge is a "daily metric" for your car. It indicates the current status (health) of your car as well as how long you can go before you run out of gas. Your business needs to be monitored the same way.

There are hundreds of options for your Daily Metrics, and a simple Yahoo search (yes, I just dissed Google) on the terms "Financial Ratios" or "Business Ratios" will give you a hundred more. The key is to find a simple number that accurately indicates your current business health and predicts the future for your cash, sales, and inventory. Other important aspects that are worthwhile but a bit more difficult to track are client satisfaction, employee morale, and other non-tangible aspects of your business.

You don't need to do the obvious here, either. You're going for metrics that indicate current and future health. And you want to make it as easy as possible to collect the data. For example, with my first company we tracked the number of times a new call came into our company the previous day. It didn't matter if it was from a vendor, client, cold call, or even if it was a misdial. We simply tracked how many calls came in a day. Our receptionist had a clicker and would click it every time someone called.

So why was that important? We determined that our call volume tied into our sales, since over time a certain percentage of the calls were new prospects. A certain percentage of those prospects became customers. And those customers sent us money. So every day we would report the call number. Over time we learned that a call volume of 3000 calls in a 30-day rolling period would result in about $150K in monthly sales three months later. This became a very powerful indicator, since we could predict our sales three months in advance simply by the phone ringing. You can imagine the power of knowing what your sales are going to be three months from now – you can prepare smartly and manage your cash better. That is the power of metrics.

One note: The Daily Metrics will change over time, and may change radically, but typically will not change more than once a quarter. As I said before, the Daily Metrics need to blend your Prosperity Plan and the current Quarterly Plan. When first starting out, you may have all your focus on sales, so your Daily Metrics relate predominantly to sales. As you grow and bring on new colleagues, your Daily Metrics may shift to reflect morale or performance factors. Daily Metrics are meant to reflect the health of the company, and over time you will want to monitor other parts of the corporate body.

Here is a snapshot of what our Daily Metrics may look like on any given day:

Obsidian Launch's Daily Metrics

Cash Capacity	Partner Revenue (Prior Day)	Partner Testimonials (Prior Day)	Speaking Engagements (Rolling 30)	Application Review (Prior Day)
Cash	Sales	Service	Marketing	Administration
3.7	$72.3K	24	8	2.4 hr
+	+	-	-	+

The Daily Metrics are the most effective way of keeping your finger on the pulse of your company. Studies have shown that when there is an acute focus on a specific number, the number improves. That's the power of keeping your finger on the pulse.

(Yes, you can download a sample of this, too, at www.ToiletPaper-Entrepreneur.com.)

Gold Bullion Everywhere

In the introduction to this book, I mention how emotion is a key factor in absorbing and retaining information. While powerful, re-membering to use the Daily Metrics as a tool may be challenging for you and your staff.

At Lawline, an Internet-based source for Continuing Legal Educa-tion (CLE), the Daily Metrics are in the forefront of the minds of every employee. Why? Because they have a visual example that hits them emotionally every time they see it.

Lawline's President, David Schnurman, came up with the idea to motivate his staff using a display case full of gold bullion. Each bul-lion bar represents $10K in annual revenue. As sales accumulate, new bars are added to the stack. A great concept, but here's the ge-nius of David's idea: every time the company sales reach one million, *every staff member is handed a real, solid gold bar.* That's visual! That's emotional!

Employees pass by the gold-bullion display in Lawline's reception area several times a day. This keeps them in a near-constant state of awareness of the company's daily metric for revenue. How does this system translate to cold, hard cash? Since implementing this powerful visual and emotional reminder of the company's Daily Metrics, Lawline has seen a 600% growth in revenue! David attributes a significant portion of his company's growth to his method of presenting his daily metrics. David Schnurman is a Toilet Paper Entrepreneur.

It's Just Like Driving to Albuquerque

Let's say you live in Loco Hills, New Mexico, and want to travel to the big city of Albuquerque. To get started you would probably figure out exactly where you are going in Albuquerque, whether you are taking a car or bus, how long it will take, where you will stay, and the roads you plan to travel to get there.

The planning required for taking a trip is identical to the intention of the Prosperity Plan. It details the vehicle you will drive (Life Mission), your destination, and the time you anticipate it will take to get there (Destiny); the roads you will travel (Area of Innovation), the rules of the road (Immutable Laws), and with whom you will be traveling (Community).

As you set out from Loco Hills up good old US-82, you will only be able to see as far as the next turn in front of you. As you travel, 99% of your time will be spent looking out the windshield and making decisions to safely, quickly, and legally get to the next turn. This is identical to the intention of the Quarterly Plan. Just as when driving your car, you need to focus your attention on the road as far as the next turn, avoiding obstacles, adjusting to problems, and most of the time just keeping the steering wheel steady and the gas pedal properly depressed.

During your travels from US-82 all the way to your destination on Interstate 40, you regularly take quick peeks at the fuel gauge, speedometer, and other indicators to make sure all things are as expected. If you start running low on gas, you find the next exit to fill up. This is identical to your Daily Metrics, where you constantly check the fuel, speed, and health of your overall business.

Use the Prosperity Plan, Quarterly Plan, and the Daily Metrics to constantly grow your company the right way. This method is a million times more effective than any business plan and is way more dynamic. It is amazing what you can do with three sheets of paper and some numbers.

TPE TIP

Research – While you're at the library, check out the reference desk. Reference librarians know where to find *everything*. Best of all, they love a challenge. Don't pay for research. Do some yourself and get the reference librarians to help with the rest. Find out where your state library is located, because there you will find top-notch research material, including extensive mailing lists and statistical information.

TAKE ACTION NOW!

If you read through this entire chapter, you can probably guess what your three action steps are. Again, your "three sheets" are living documents; you can always come back and tweak them later on.

1. If you haven't finished it yet (or even started it), create your Prosperity Plan. Remember, it better make you bawl out loud or it's not going to sustain you through those lean, mean, early days of launching a business.

2. Next, bang out a Quarterly Plan. Keep it simple and realistic. Even if there are only two days left in the quarter, don't wait for the next one. You'll be amazed at how much you can get done just because you said you would.

3. Establish Daily Metrics for your business. Think outside the box to come up with a visual example that will keep you motivated and on track.

PART THREE:
Action

"One worthwhile task carried to a successful conclusion
is worth half-a-hundred half-finished tasks."
– Malcolm S. Forbes

The strategy has been laid out for you. You appreciate the criticality of an enabling mindset and have set the wheels in motion to build it. You have the plans in place and know exactly where you are headed. You know what you need to do in the next ninety days to get there. Now there is one thing left. It's show time. It's time to put all of this stuff into action.

Since you are reading this book, I must assume you are perched on the edge of starting your first business or seeking ways to greatly improve a company you are floundering with. This is a scary time. Either way, you are facing actions and decisions that you have never made before.

Even with your new TPE knowledge and TPE tools, the comfort of your past is powerful and alluring. The familiarity of repeating past actions, albeit unsuccessful ones, can seem much safer than moving decisively down an unexplored path.

Until we take a leap of faith, none of us know if we can fly. But isn't it better to leave the repeated failures behind once and for all and move decisively toward change, rather than sit on the sidelines wondering if you can do it? Aren't you tired of seeing others succeed while you continue a life of mediocrity? And isn't a life of mediocrity, well, mediocre?

It's your turn now. It's time to boldly step forward to an amazing life of entrepreneurship. It's time to take the leap. But don't worry; I am not here to push you off the edge. I plan to THROW you off.

CHAPTER 6 – ARE YOU READY NOW?

"Up, sluggard, and waste not life;
in the grave will be sleeping enough."
– Benjamin Franklin

First, let me dispel a great myth. There is a common misconception circulating around that says if you don't exit the womb with entrepreneurial drive then you're done; or at least, you will never be able to achieve levels that natural-born entrepreneurs can. While I agree that your desire is part of you from birth, just because you haven't discovered it in yourself yet does not mean it's not there. Your entrepreneurial drive could be somewhere deep inside you, dormant, waiting for you to find it.

Most people get entrepreneurial inspiration in a flash, kind of a "what if" moment, as it were. Personally, mine came during a drunken stupor a few years after graduating from college. The point is, it doesn't matter when it hits you, be it in college, soon thereafter, or when you're ninety years old. What does matter is that you take action. If you don't take action, your drive may wane for awhile, only to come back years later and bite you in the ass. The Toilet Paper Entrepreneur knows that when the urge hits, it is go time.

"No" Your Way to Success

Until you close some doors, it's impossible to open others! Great business growth requires saying "No" way more often than you say "Yes."

Here's a question for the guys: I don't mean to offend anyone here (too much), but who are the most desired girls? The ones you can't have, right? Not the girls who are ho'ing around. You sure as heck don't want to be in a long-term relationship with one of those loose chicks. Who knows what (or whom) she will be doing behind your back? Plus, you can get some gross diseases that way.

It's probably the same for girls, right? You want a great, non-creepy guy who is going to stick around and be committed, not the guy who is with every girl at the party. I know, I know, some people like the challenge of "taming" the bad boy or the bad girl, but how many of those relationships work long term? Squat, that's how many.

So do you want to be known as the industry whore, doing any project for anybody at any price, just because you think you have to stay busy to grow? Be selective. Otherwise, you'll get a reputation, and none of the decent businesses or partners will want to get into bed with you. Turn away projects that are best suited for someone else and those that are not in line with the beliefs outlined in your Prosperity Plan. Start saying "No" to grow.

If you have been shortchanged, ripped off, taken advantage of, unfairly pressured, squeezed, or even underappreciated by a client, the problem is yours to fix, not his. You must commit to saying "No" to all of those crappy clients, bottom-feeding prospects, and unfit opportunities this year. Seriously, right now, get on your knees, look up to the sky, and swear you will start saying "No." Don't worry, no one is looking at you. Did you do it? Did you get on your knees? No?!? Good! You are learning to say "No." But if you did do that little exercise, start this section over. You clearly haven't learned the lesson. You. Yes, you!

Saying "No" is all about sustaining your absolute focus. If you haven't grasped this yet, I am going to continue ramming it down your throat: *Your success is entirely contingent upon your foundation of enabling beliefs, your relentless focus, and your actions consistent with those beliefs and focus.*

When you are starting and growing a business, the unimportant stuff keeps creeping in – the distractions, from reading every email every second it comes in (and clicking the send/receive button a hundred time just to check), to constant instant messaging fests, to "working" on "opportunities" that are not in your niche, to time-chewing meetings that don't help anyone. You need to say "No" to this stuff and focus on what is important.

Another cool thing about saying "No" to certain people is that they become hungrier. They want what they can't have. A classic example is alcohol consumption among teenagers. It is chic to have what you are not allowed. So even though booze is illegal to anyone under 21 in the US, teenagers represent a huge consumer base for the alcohol industry. You will find in your own business that certain clients you tell "No" will come back with a better, more fitting proposition, and you may suddenly find yourself happily saying "YES."

Today's most successful companies have been influenced more by what they have said "No" to than what they have said "Yes" to. Think about this for a moment. Allow it to sink in. If you're nervous about this, I get it. When you're just starting out in business, it may seem crazy to say "No" to anyone. How are you supposed to grow your business if you turn people away?

For two years I served on the board of the Young Entrepreneurs Organization (now called EO) and was responsible for growing the membership of our local chapter. Both years I won the award for facilitating one of the three fastest-growing chapters in the world (out of 100). For the ten years prior to that, the chapter had grown about 0.5% per year. I bumped that number up to 75% growth per year.

You know what I did differently than the guy before me? I said, "No." I limited admission, telling prospective members they had to pass an approval process to qualify for membership. I rejected everyone the first time around, and those who were eventually accepted couldn't wait to pay the membership fee. That is the power of saying "No."

TPE TIP

Phone – Use VOIP (Voice Over IP) phones. These phones connect to your computer or are stand-alone units and use the Internet to dial out. Skype.com is one of the best resources and Skype-to-Skype calls are free.

The Top Nine List

Joe Spano, President of Buy-Rite, Inc., took his twenty-five-year-old stagnant business and increased annual revenue by 60% in two years just by saying "No." What he did wasn't complex; the whole plan fit on a single poster board. Joe's strategy didn't cost a dime; it simply required a new mindset.

It all started when Joe recognized that his team was in a constant scramble to satisfy the needs of its one hundred key clients, and that the company's beliefs were compromised. They wanted to do more, faster, but with so many priority clients, it just wasn't working. Joe realized it was impossible to have one hundred key clients. It's like saying you have one hundred best friends. It's just not possible.

Joe and his colleagues took action immediately, developing a customer ranking strategy founded on three simple questions:

1. Is the customer already a significant annual revenue-producer or, if not, does the customer have a realistic potential to become one?

2. Will the customer commit to scheduled and frequent communications with Buy-Rite to discuss its needs?

3. Does the addition of this customer to the key list significantly improve the overall synergy of the entire group?

With this list of three vital questions, Joe's team sorted and identified its list of one hundred key clients and culled it down to nine. The Top Nine was posted above every desk in every office, from the receptionist's to the CEO's. Buy-Rite then committed, with no exception, to do everything possible to say "Yes" to all requests from the Top Nine.

More importantly, it said "No" to every other customer every time that customer's needs were not one hundred percent consistent with the needs of the Top Nine. In Joe's words, "We essentially built our business around the needs of nine customers, not everyone's needs. We became truly SPECIFIC customer driven. All other customers were simply extensions of these Top Nine. If they did not like that, we lost them and we were prepared to accept that."

Within one month of implementing the new strategy, Buy-Rite replaced one of the Top Nine, and it wasn't just any company. It was Wal-Mart. Yes, the biggest retailer in the world was removed from Buy-Rite's Top Nine client list because it did not pass requirement number two (communication).

By saying "No" to the majority and "Yes" to a small minority, Buy-Rite experienced skyrocketing revenue growth. But that's not all. The benefits to the Top Nine were so effective, they trickled down to the other clients, who also bought more, driving a 10% increase in revenue from that client sector.

By far the most impressive benefit was the bottom line. This new mindset resulted in a profit increase of 250%. That is a lot of cold hard cash. With a new mindset, business boomed. It really, really boomed. Joe's once-sluggish company achieved sales of $19M only two years after implementing the Top Nine strategy. It was on pace for $25M in sales during the third year, when Buy-Rite was snapped up by an investment group seeking fast-growth companies.

All that success from saying "No." Joe Spano is a Toilet Paper Entrepreneur.

The Dark Side

Experience is nature's way of teaching us the results to expect when we behave in a certain way. When it comes to many of life's situations, experience is an invaluable asset. Think about grabbing a scalding hot iron. Do it once, or observe someone else doing it, and your experience will clearly remind you never to do it again. That's a good thing. But experience has a dark side, too. We anticipate results based on our experience when, in fact, the same results may never happen again. While our experience indicates a danger, there may be no danger at all. Experience stopped me from eating French toast for over a decade! Experience may stop you before you start.

A danger of having prior business experience is that it may cloud your vision and cause you to use outdated strategies when what's really needed is a new approach. Like a lemming, you follow your experience and rigid business fundamentals right off the ledge to your death.

Things are changing so quickly in business that if you are adhering to experiences from a mere five years ago, the world has already passed you by and lapped you a few times. Entrepreneurs who master and adhere to core business/life principles, such as treat others the way you would like to be treated, succeed because they make decisions based on their value systems, not the almighty dollar or "expert" opinion. Those entrepreneurs who adhere to life principles AND constantly adapt to elusive business dynamics experience *enormous*, lasting success.

Never started a company before? Walking into it with no preconceived notions? No baseline to judge your progress against? Thank God! You've got a shot at making this work.

Haven't Been There, Haven't Done That

If you actually knew everything that would be expected and required of you to start your own business, you might actually be smart enough not to do it. That would be a shame.

Imagine if the Founding Fathers of the United States thought about every variable and planned out every detail of the American Revolution. If they had thought it through, they surely would have known it was foolish even to try.

Let's see here, the British have a far larger army, their forces are much better equipped, they have tons of money, they have tremendous amounts of war experience, and they are motivated to keep us in their kingdom. In comparison, we have no army at all and will need to make one, we don't have uniforms or adequate equipment, not many people really support the cause, we don't have our own currency, and this will be our first war.

Now let's get into the details. We need to attack the British here, then run over there and attack them. We will need to do crazy stuff such as cross frozen rivers, attack the British on Christmas day, and use a marginal general (named George) to lead a lot of the battles. As things move along, we must convince other countries to come help us fight. If we win, George must become President, not King, and relinquish a lot of his power to others. And then, when this is done, we need to make England our key ally going forward. What's a knock-down, drag out death match among friends?

If they really started to dig into the details and figure out each step, they would have determined it was a hopeless fight and given up before it started. That would have been the smart thing to do.

Instead of an elaborate plan, the Founding Fathers had a crystal vision and a purpose in the Declaration of Independence, which they wrote early in the war and used to attract the support of people who shared the same values. This document, this final commitment, put America on the course to kick ass.

The Americans took their cause, step by grueling step, through an ever-changing, dynamic process. After each win and each loss, their short-term plan was adjusted to be in alignment with the envisioned future. Success was due to simple planning, unwavering focus, and letting the bullets fly right away.

The impossible become very possible because the Founding Fathers weren't bogged down by what they didn't need to know. They hadn't been there and they hadn't done that. Thank God. The learning and the tweaks and the changes all happened as they moved along. The only constant was their vision.

TPE TIP

Sales/Marketing Automation – Even if you are a sales force of one, you can appear to be much more sophisticated than that. And you can do it for free. Try Zoho CRM. It offers a free package when you have three users or less. Could be a perfect way for you to compete with the big boys.

What You Don't Know Can't Pervert You

This title is a bit of a stretch. I went for the play on words here. When I use the word pervert in this context, I mean to stray away from the proper course. Got it? Good. Now work with me, you pervert.

Not too long ago my father planned to tile his kitchen. Overall, it was a relatively simple project, minus a couple corner turns. The planning stage went from a few hours to a few days. Then his engineer mind went into overdrive, and the detailed investigation went on for weeks. He wanted to make sure that every element was addressed and even set up a mock layout using the actual tile in his dining room.

Every day the planning became more and more intricate. One small problem would be resolved, but it would cause two more micro adjustments. Those adjustments would yield the need for more change.

Finally, the day came to install the tile. So guess what happened? Right! The tile didn't fit. The corners were not calculated correctly, and he had to pull up the tile and do it again. But this time he executed a basic plan and an ultimate goal, not a detailed step-by-step action guide.

When I asked him about the failed project, my father taught me a lesson I will never forget. "I over-thought it," he said. Then he called me a nosey bastard. He experienced the result of over-processing something, of thinking too much about it. It was in this über-planning that he "discovered" umpteen paths that perverted him from achieving the original goal.

Here is a little bit of a paradox. Properly executing a process is all about doing it first, then planning for it. The first time through is often best served with less planning and more doing. The first time through is about dynamic adjustment and improvement as you execute. Only after you've successfully completed the process is it time to get into the details. Why after? Because now you need to make it repeatable; you need to ensure that it can be done to the same standards the same way every time. It must become measurable. As the process is repeated over and over by something or someone other than you, your job becomes constant observation and improvement.

Yes, the devil is in the details, but you will have a devil of a time getting anything done the first go around if you fixate on them. So when it comes to process, rough-cut a plan for the first job, but don't try to anticipate the details of unfamiliar territory. Use the experience to learn and improve. *Then* get into the details for the next go around and master a repeatable process.

Anyone know a good tile guy?

Burn the Boats

This is a story that has been floating around for centuries. True or not, it holds a powerful lesson.

A young military leader faced a situation that required him to ensure the success of a critical battle. A loss would have resulted in the collapse of his military, a tragic ending to the war. The leader's situation was made worse by that fact that he was facing an opponent who had him greatly outnumbered, was positioned defensively (often the superior position in a fight) and had the advantage of better equipment.

Unshaken, the leader loaded his soldiers onto ships, sailed to the enemy's shores and unloaded his soldiers and equipment. He then gave the order to burn the boats that had just carried them. Addressing his men before they set out to battle, he said, "You see the boats going up in flames? That means the only way we can leave this land alive is if we are victorious! We have no options. We win, or we perish!"

They won.

You must do the same in your entrepreneurial endeavor. You must cut off all the alternatives and put your entire being into the success of your new company. By burning away any and all methods of retreat, you will focus your mind and body on moving forward. This is essential to a successful launch. Go burn your boats. That is, unless your business is selling boats.

TAKE ACTION NOW!

Compared to the last two sets of action steps, these three exercises will be a breeze! I'm gonna say twenty minutes, tops.

1. Think about times in your life when you said "Yes" and really should have said "No." How would your life be different today if you had gone with your gut?

2. Identify your key customers, the people and businesses that make up most of your revenue and also make you feel good about doing business with them. How could you structure your business in a way that would allow you to say "No" to those people and businesses who are not key customers or who do not fit with your Prosperity Plan?

3. How has inexperience been an asset in your life and in your business? How has it been a liability?

CHAPTER 7 – SHIT AND GET OFF THE POT

"You see, in life, lots of people know what to do,
but few people actually do what they know.
Knowing is not enough! You must take action."
– Anthony Robbins

W hen it comes to action there is only one lesson. Start now. There really isn't much else to say. Start now! Start now! Start now! (Yes, I am stomping around like a bratty girl right now.)

Many people talk a big game of business and entrepreneurialism but continue their routine of uninspired existence, never taking the leap. This is what separates the men from the boys and the women from the girls. You have to take action. You have to revel in the possibility of failure, since it is the springboard to success. The only true failure is never to have tried, and those who refuse to try are just plain stupid.

Colin Powell once shared knowledge we can all benefit from, a formula to determine when to take action. Simply put, he uses a metric called P = 40 to 70, where P stands for the probability of success and the numbers indicate the percentage of information acquired so far. Once 40% to 70% of the knowledge is collected and probability of success is at least 40%, you are at the decision point of action. Go with your gut and then take immediate action.

This means that you should always have enough information to support your theories, but if you sit around waiting for all the information and the probability of success to be 100%, it will be too late.

The Secret Behind The Secret

Have you seen the movie *The Secret*? The documentary where they present the hermetic law of attraction? Great movie! If you haven't seen it yet, drop this book right now and go get it.

I believe that the law of attraction exists and works, but damn it, they missed on the action component. I wonder how many people sat on their couch expecting money, love, and fame but never lifted a finger to get it. Those are surely some very disappointed people. Sure, if you focus on something you will inevitably see it. The problem is you've got to grab it, mold it, leverage it, use it, and make it happen.

Here is the secret behind *The Secret*: When you truly want something and are passionate about it, the work that you must do to achieve what you want is often fun, energizing, and/or easy. When you are doing what you love to do and are pursuing what you want, the actions are obvious. Getting started is often the most difficult part.

Once you have the beliefs and the focus, the final ingredient is action. Don't worry about making mistakes. In fact, the more mistakes you make, the more progress you are making. Just don't repeat the same mistakes. Of course, you are making progress with each success as well. The only way to *not* make progress is to sit still and do nothing. So gleefully accept your mistakes and learn from them. Celebrate your successes and learn to achieve them more easily the next time. Mistakes are good, successes are great, and idleness is a sin.

TPE TIP

Staff – Some retired folks want to work just to have somewhere to go. You may be surprised by how many people want to volunteer just to stay busy and have some fun. Ask around. I bet you Mom, Dad, and Uncle Billy wouldn't mind pitching in a little. Or recruit some eager interns to help you out. During the summer, college students sign up with University of Dreams to intern in industries they aspire to work in when they graduate. Check it out.

Just in Case You Haven't Started Yet, Here's How

It's not enough to simply say that you should take action; you actually need to do it. Even if your actions are not greatly productive at first, at least you are doing something. Yapping about your ideas and dreams doesn't count; get off your ass and get moving. Here are a few tricks to get you started:

Capture Your Action Items – As the ideas or thoughts of what you need to do cross your mind, write them down on a list. There is comfort in knowing you have a record of what needs to be done. That alone can help you focus and start taking action.

Prioritize – A lot of things you need to do are small, quick items, but they can swallow up time just by wasting an eternity winding up and down from them. Prioritize a list of the important stuff first and group together the smaller stuff to be done in one shot later. Or better yet, have someone else do the smaller stuff.

Eliminate Duplicates – Sometimes I have prioritized my lists only to realize that several tasks have only slight variations. If I find duplicates, I blend the work together and start banging away. Do you have tasks with certain actions in common? Do them in one shot.

If it Only Takes Two, Do – Sometimes tasks are so simple and quick that the time you would take to get them recorded and prioritized would take longer than just doing them in the first place. If you have tasks that clearly can be completed in under two minutes, do them right away. Don't waste any time trying to manage these things.

Eliminate Time-Wasters – Some tasks just aren't worth it. Scratch them off your list and forget about them. Don't delegate them to someone else either, and waste her time. If it's a waste of time, it's a waste of time.

Concentrate Your Thoughts – Instead of clouding your mind with rambling thoughts, stop for a moment and focus on one thing. Think about it repeatedly and then tear into it. This isn't as hard as it sounds. Ever hear a tune and can't get it out of your head? It's because you listened to the song closely when you heard it, repeated it in your head, and it became an overwhelming focus.

Turn Off the Email – This was one of my biggest problems. Even though I set my email to check once every three hours, I caught myself clicking send/receive every ten seconds. Check email only twice a day – around lunch and again at the end of day. In between, turn it off. Make it inaccessible. You will get a lot more work done that way. I do.

Delegate – Whenever possible give the work you are not great at to someone else who is great at it. This does not mean giving up your accountability for the work; it just means you assign someone else the responsibility of completing the task. You still need to check on the progress, but you don't need to do it or micromanage it. Delegate everything you can, abdicate nothing.

Commit to Someone Else – When the task at hand needs to be delivered to a third party, it will get your butt in gear. So tie your tasks into deliverables. When other people depend on you, you will deliver. Commit to a deadline and backtrack to the actions you must complete to meet your commitment. Then take them. The pressure of having someone else depending on you will definitely keep you moving forward.

Make it Manageable – Some tasks are way too big to be done in a single sitting or even in a short time frame. These big tasks need to be broken down into bite-sized pieces that can be accomplished quickly. It is much easier to take action when you can see a step through to completion, take a break if needed, and then move on to the next. I once asked a brain surgeon how difficult her work was. She said that anyone could perform brain surgery because it is an extremely simple process. The only challenge is getting each of the five hundred simple steps done completely and in the right order.

Take a Break – Once you are in the groove, taking action and getting stuff done, realize that you will get tired at some point. You'll start drifting off-focus, and your productivity will wane. That's OK. It's actually more than OK. It's your signal to take a break. So do it, take a break.

Go in Spurts – Many people perform better by working in shorter segments, taking a break from the action, and then starting up again.

Try it. Go into a task with the promise that you will both take breaks as needed and get right back to it when break time is over.

Reward Yourself - When I finish a task, I love to put a line through it on my list. When I look at the list I see all the stuff I have done. It feels great to complete so much. Sometimes I buy myself a treat. Whatever works for you, do it. Make sure you reward yourself.

Make Failure VERY Painful – You won't grab an iron if you know it is going to burn the living crap out of you. You will also complete a task if failure to do so results in the same scalding burn. Since I don't suggest you motivate yourself with the threat of physical pain, money can be a great motivator. Give a $100 bill to a friend and tell him it's his to keep if you don't complete the task at hand. You'll complete the task! And, like any true friend, he will have already spent the money by the time you're finished.

Stop Your Bitching, Bitch – At some point, enough is enough. If you still aren't taking any action, you should just be embarrassed with yourself. Look in the mirror, acknowledge you have been a pathetic loser to this point, and stop the bullshit now, bitch. Get your ass in gear and starting doing it. Yes, that's right, I called you a bitch.

Action, Lights, Camera

Fred DeLuca, founder of Subway, built one of the world's most successful restaurant chains, which by 2004 had achieved over $5 billion in sales with 15,000 restaurants in 76 countries. To have success like that you better go in with a plan, right? Not if you are Fred DeLuca.

With a $1,000 investment, Fred opened his inaugural store in 1965. When the first customer walked in the door to buy a sub sandwich, Fred realized he didn't know how to make it. That's right; he opened his first sandwich shop, greeted his first customer, and didn't even plan how to make a sandwich. What he did do was take action despite improper and incomplete preparation. The result, in his case, was five big bills.

I am not suggesting you launch your business blindly. As you have learned, you need a complete understanding of your beliefs and your focus. You need to have a good idea of what you are doing and how you plan to do it. But you also know that you can't be 100% prepared for everything, nor should you be. If you work hard and work smart, the actions you take will more than compensate for any poor planning.

Don't wait for the lights to be on and the cameras to start rolling. It might be too late then. Oh yeah, did I mention that Fred DeLuca was seventeen years old when he started Subway? Fred DeLuca is a Toilet Paper Entrepreneur. You can be one, too. Take action. Start now!

Happily Walk Out of a Once-in-a-Lifetime Meeting

Once a year a group of leading business thinkers, world-renowned business authors and cream-of-the-crop, cutting-edge entrepreneurs from all over the world gather at MIT in Boston for five, fourteen-plus-hour days of intense learning and idea exchange. The "Birthing of Giants" group, also jokingly referred to as "The Gathering of Egos," is extremely difficult to join, and the cost is not cheap. If you are lucky enough to participate, you better bring your A game, and it goes without saying that you don't leave before it's over. That is unless you're Barrett Ersek of Happy Lawn.

The first full day's session is always extremely intense. It kicks off with mind-blowing concepts, over-the-edge experiences, horrible crash-and-burn stories and amazing try-and-fly stories. Everyone hangs on the edge of his seat, jotting notes as fast as possible, laptops clicking away. You don't dare take a premature break for the bathroom; there is too much powerful information being shared. It's better to have your eyeballs floating than to leave the room.

Forty-five minutes in and rolling, Barrett Ersek jumped up in front of the group of about seventy people and said, "I gotta go!" Another member shouted out the thoughts of the group, "Good for you, the bathroom is down the hallway. Now shut up." Everyone's focus returned to the discussion at hand.

"No, you don't get it. I gotta go. I just figured out a key strategy for my business. I gotta go now and get to work on it," Barret explained. A normal group would tell him he was crazy, how much these meetings cost, and what a waste of money it was to leave. Everyone knows you can do it next week. But this is not a normal group. Instead, Barrett got a standing ovation. He left, bought a dictation machine at a local store, and drove from Boston to Philadelphia, dictating his ideas the entire way. He started on his project that night. Talk about taking action now! That is how you do it.

So what was the idea? What if he could get a proposal to a customer in minutes, not days, without the need to ever go onsite?

Let me explain. Barrett's company is in the lawn care industry, competing against franchises such as ChemLawn. The challenge in the industry is in the proposal stage. If someone wants an estimate for lawn care, vendors like Barrett first dispatch a lawn care specialist to measure the property and examine the landscape. A lot of time and money goes into preparing an estimate, and if you do get the contract it takes two or three lawn treatments to recoup the cost of preparing the estimate.

At that non-ideal, crazy moment Barrett had an idea that was amazing. He wondered if he could use satellite images, like the ones in Google Maps, to measure the properties and review the landscapes without ever going onsite. This idea may have crossed other people's minds, but Barrett did what many never do. He took action immediately.

With new, patent-pending technology, Barrett's company increased sales by $10M in a little over two years, a feat that had taken Barrett and his team seven years to achieve in the past. Costs dropped and profits were up. A lot. Barrett Ersek is a Toilet Paper Entrepreneur.

Action is the only way to make progress. Take action now; don't wait for a convenient time. It can't be overemphasized. Take action now. Throw this book down right now and take action!

Act As If, But Only on the Inside

When it comes time to take action, sometimes you don't know *how* to act. Maybe you have to make that big sales call and close the deal. Maybe you are hiring your first employee. What are the actions you need to take? How do you do it?

Though the execution may be a challenge, the answer is simple. In short, you need to act internally (in your mind) as if you have already achieved what you want, AND you must act outwardly in the way you would want to be treated once you arrive at your destination.

This is not the "act as if" message you saw in *Boiler Room*. I once had a guy call on me to sell me a phone system I needed. I distinctly remember the absolute attitude this schmuck had. He knew the proper answers and was persistent. He was behaving like he had already achieved his goals by "assuming the sale."

Using the old school method of sales, he was following the ABC's (Always Be Closing). He was using phrases like, "Do you want us to deliver the phone system today or tomorrow?" Even though I had not ordered the system from him, he kept on with questions like, "I appreciate your commitment to this system, would you prefer a one-time payment or monthly installments?" I thought he was a jackass, politely got out of the meeting, and was grateful NOT to have a phone system from someone like him.

The phone system salesperson was only executing half of a successful sales strategy, and even that part was screwed up. Yes, he was **technically** "acting as if," but he was doing it outwardly through words and gestures, not inwardly through confidence. When you "act as if" in your mind, the actions come through as confidence.

The second component to successfully "acting as if" is that your outward actions need to be consistent with how you envision the ideal prospect would want those actions to play out. Put yourself in the shoes of the person on the other side. What would "wow" you? Treat the other person that way, and then some.

Never "assume the sale," a horrible strategy from 1950. Instead, proceed with the internal confidence of having already made the sale, but behave outwardly with the decency of an exceptional human

TPE TIP

Business Mentoring – The Service Corps of Retired Executives (SCORE) maintains a large group of been-there, done-that business executives who provide business mentoring to start ups for free. They'll match you with two or three former execs that know your specific industry, and they are in regular contact with the Small Business Administration (SBA), so if you are going for an SBA loan, they can help. Many of these individuals also have key contacts who may further help your business grow. Check out Score.org for more information.

being. You'll be able to sleep well at night, and chances are you'll get the sale.

Here's what "acting as if" definitely is not. It's not lying. Some people take "acting as if" to an extreme and go on a lying spree. Spewing lies of their greatness and success. That is the worst thing you can do. When people find you out, and they will, they will lose trust in you. Soon you'll have people talking trash about you or your company behind your back and avoiding you at all costs.

Acting "as if" is all about making a vision for yourself of what you want to achieve, a clear picture of how the person you **want to be** would act in a certain situation. It's all about being truthful to yourself and others about where you are heading and who you are now.

The 16,107 Steps You (Don't) Need to Take

While looking at my bookshelf bowing under the weight of tons of business books, I noticed that many of them had titles such as *The 13 Way to Do This*, *1,000 Tricks To That*, and *The 7 Strategies For Whatever*. How could they all be right?

I decided to do some informal research. I went on Amazon to determine the number of actions, in total, that the world's business, personal success, and financial books said we needed to know in order to successfully start, grow, and maintain our businesses and our lives. I lost count at 16,107. Absolutely absurd!

For example, one book claims there are *100 Absolutely Unbreakable Laws to Business Success* (Brian Tracy), another book says that there are *601 Essential Things That Everyone in Business Needs* (Barbara Pachter), and yet another asserts there are *28 Sure Fire Strategies for Business and Personal Success* (Tom Leonard & Byron Larson). Or how about the book that states the *7 Irrefutable Laws That Determine Business Success* (David Eichenbaum)? Yet none of them are identical to the *16 Lessons in the Law of Success* (Napoleon Hill).

So which book is right? Which book do I follow? How can they all be "unbreakable," "irrefutable," and "essential?" And how the hell am I going to do 16,107 things without going completely insane? Arrgh! This is confusing!

It gets even worse when it comes to managing your colleagues at your new growing business. Did you know there are *1,001 Ways to Reward Employees* (Bob Nelson), yet only *365 Way to Motivate (Dianna Podmoroff)* them, *151 Ideas to Recognize Them (Ken Lloyd)*, and a meager *150 Ways to Inspire Them* (Donna Deeprose)? So if you get the formula mixed up, you may end up trying to motivate yourself to inspire them to reward no one, and you won't even be recognized for your effort. Crap!

So what is the right answer? How many different actions do you need to take to be successful? There is no magic formula, but the number of actions can easily be in the tens or hundreds of thousands. While I like to bust the chops of these books, they all revolve around the truth of one foundational principle:

Belief + Focus = Apparent Action

Don't get inundated by over-thinking the various steps and process-es. So many people get overwhelmed trying to decide which steps are the right ones. Quite frankly, even just seven steps to success are still too many to juggle at once. Tips and advice serve you best when you seek them out as relevant issues come up and not before.

Here are the ONLY five things you need to do to succeed in any-thing:

1. Determine what you want.

2. Set an enabling belief.

3. Commit focus and attention to your goal.

4. Take the most obvious actions to achieve your goal.

5. Monitor your progress, adjusting your actions to realign with your goal.

So instead of worrying and preparing for all the different actions that may or may not be required of you, set a foundation for action first.

With the right enabling belief and focus, the required actions will become apparent. When consulting all of those business and personal growth books, use your gut to identify the actions, ideas, and solutions to build on what you intuitively know is true.

Know When to Say When

In 1992, Scott Allen, Founder of The Windows Experts, thought he had timing on his side. The U.S. economy was just starting to crawl out of a recession, and the demand for Windows-based computer networks was about to go through the roof. Scott was steeped in Windows networking knowledge, carrying expert certifications and experience that was unmatched. The competition was weak and unfocused due to the quiet times of the recession. Demand was growing faster than supply. Opportunity was knocking. Scott jumped on it and started The Windows Experts.

Within weeks of his launch clients started coming on board. But many were small clients, and the sporadic demand did not suit a scalable business. Scott pursued big clients, and when the State of Texas seemed to have the perfect mix of long-term projects, Scott dumped his small clients in order to work exclusively with the big guys. Along with his growing business came a heftier bottom line, so when, just weeks into the new projects, the State of Texas reorganized and abruptly cut off The Windows Experts and other vendors, Scott was in trouble.

The loss of his biggest client put a huge damper on Scott's business, and he no longer had small clients to fall back on. With two teens and a newborn at home, Scott and his wife took a serious look at the business and their future. Their analysis changed the course of his business permanently.

Scott and his wife calculated it would take three to six months to reestablish the business with small clients. They discussed the sacrifices of starting over, such as no family time. And they talked about Scott's passion. Did he have enough drive to pull the business out of the hole? Did he want it badly enough? Considering the numbers, the sacrifices, and Scott's lack of sufficient interest in his business, the choice was obvious. It was time to stop.

After Scott called it quits, he accepted a full-time position that took care of his financial needs and allowed him time to discover a passion worth fighting for. A few years later, he found it. Based on his love of transforming virtual relationships into real relationships, Scott launched Link to Your World. Today, Scott is one of the leading authorities on the topic of entrepreneurialism, a frequent speaker on social media, and a fixture on Google's front page for the keyword "entrepreneur." No easy feat. That is unless you know when to stop and rediscover your passion. Scott Allen is a Toilet Paper Entrepreneur.

Accountability

When Toilet Paper Entrepreneurs get down to business, they take full accountability for their situation and the job in front of them. It was their responsibility to check for a full roll of TP ahead of time. If there are only three sheets left, it's their own fault. Weaker minds will blame the other guy for not replacing it. The Toilet Paper Entrepreneur takes responsibility every step of the way.

Where you are today is a direct result of your decisions. You are accountable for your success, and you are accountable for your failures. If you are pointing fingers at others, you are simply building a wall of more limiting beliefs, and your actions will be stymied. Just because you were brought up poor or silver-spooned or went to a crap school or were ignored or picked on or were considered ugly or pretty or were held back or pushed forward does not excuse you from anything. All that stuff is meaningless, except that it brought you to where you are today.

Moving forward is not based upon your past; your future is exclusively determined by the decisions you make now, in this moment. The first decision is to take complete and exclusive responsibility for your success. Toilet Paper Entrepreneurs accept full and complete accountability for their lives, their businesses, and their futures.

A Good Night's Rest in the Hotel Parking Lot

When you are a single mom in your early 30s with three children to raise, it is easy to give up on your dreams. Margie Aliprandi could have done just that, but instead she held herself completely accountable for her situation and its transformation. Broke, divorced, with mouths to feed and a hefty mortgage, Margie took three steps that led her to multi-millionaire status. First, she took full ownership and responsibility for her situation. Then she documented a simple vision – to keep her family in their current home – and *then* she took decisive action.

Instead of returning to the "security" of a full-time, low-paying teaching job, Margie started her own business. She launched her first

TPE TIP

Office Space – Many businesses rent office space that isn't immediately (or ever) fully occupied. If you have friends in this situation, you are in luck. If you don't, see if you can find a renter who would be willing to offer some free space in exchange for you cleaning up the office at the end of every day. If she already has a cleaning service, find some other service you can perform or a trade you can make in exchange for free office space. You may not have money, but you do have time.

company doing what she loved, educating people on how to become financially successful. She was living what she was preaching.

Unable to afford airfare, Margie would drive great distances simply to meet with prospects. One meeting alone required a forty-six hour drive from Salt Lake City to Louisville and back. During her travels, she would stop at a hotel at night to rest – but she never checked in. The parking lot served as her room, and her car was her bed. In the morning she would get dressed, put makeup on and curl her hair in a gas station bathroom. Then she would head off to a day of meetings. With her persistence and action-first attitude, the sales started coming and coming fast.

Margie took sole responsibility for her success, she maintained absolute clarity of her goal, and she took every action necessary to succeed. She made her first million by age 35 and has made that many times over since. Margie Aliprandi is a Toilet Paper Entrepreneur.

TAKE ACTION NOW!

If you're still not taking the steps necessary to launch your business, completing the following three tasks will help you get off your ass once and for all.

1. What excuses are you still nursing? What's holding you back? Time to bust those stragglers and get moving. Make a list of anything and everything that is keeping you from your goals, and then find a way around it. Use the ideas in the first part of this chapter to help you get over, around, or through any obstacles.

2. Act as if. How would you feel, behave, and react if you already accomplished all you set out to do? What type of people would you surround yourself with? What would your days be like? Would you make different decisions? Imagine yourself already there, and then act as if you are.

3. Find a trustworthy, ass-kicking friend or colleague and ask her to help you stay on track. When you're accountable to someone, it's easier to get off your ass.

PART FOUR:
Money & Equity

"Money is better than poverty,
if only for financial reasons."
\- Woody Allen

My phone rang just minutes ago. Yet another person asking me for money to launch his business. The inevitable refrain, "I need money, I can't get started without it." I get calls like this daily. They are a waste of my time. If you are making similar calls, they are a waste of your time, too.

What's the point of running a business if you can't earn a darn good living from it? The end game of entrepreneurialism is to make enough coin to live an abundant lifestyle and to continue the purpose of your business. The problem is that so many people get caught up in the money aspect that they forget everything else that's important.

It is critical that your business *makes cash*, not that it starts with it. Millions of wannabe entrepreneurs never make it off the ground because they are waiting until they have enough money. Waiting and waiting. Enough money never comes. Inevitably their dreams are suppressed and ultimately fizzle out.

Don't sit around like a bum waiting for a handout. Learn how a lack of cash can benefit your business starting today. Learn to turn having less into generating more. Learn how to bring in cash flow through your business activities, not through begging and borrowing. You have to be *active* in the process of creating cash, not waiting and wondering if it will fall into your lap.

Conventional wisdom tells us that before we can open for business, we need to raise the money outlined in a traditional business plan. I am here to tell you again that the experts are wrong. As you have learned, the design of your company is all about YOU, and if you have survived to this point without venture capital, so will your business. Besides, a lack of resources forces you to use ingenuity, a skill that will help you stay ahead of the pack for your entire run.

CHAPTER 8 – CLEAN UP ON THREE SHEETS

"Often people attempt to live their lives backwards;
they try to have more things, or more money,
in order to do more of what they want, so they will be happier."

\- Anonymous

T he planning is over and you have taken action. Your head and heart are readier than ever. You began this process by defining your beliefs and getting in the right entrepreneurial mindset. Then you identified your finish line. You created a Prosperity Plan that gives you goose bumps. You're armed with a Quarterly Plan and the Daily Metrics, which will keep you moving in the right direction. Most importantly, you have backed your beliefs and focus with committed actions. The final piece of the puzzle is money.

When we have lots of money, our appreciation for it naturally goes the way of the full roll of TP; we wipe our ass with no concern for the next time we need it. When we lack money, our appreciation for it is the same as the last squares of TP. Those few dollar bills only go so far, and we have a very acute sense of how we need to manage them. Exploit your lack of money, master cleaning up on just a few squares. Then, when your cash reserves start growing, store it away and continue to live off only the few necessary squares. Go into every situation with the minimum amount of cash required to properly navigate it, and you will start building a healthy discipline for accumulating cash.

Lack of money requires a focus that you don't need when you have funding. When you don't have money, your thoughts are focused on ways you can navigate around that perceived obstacle. If you properly apply your focus, you will use the lack of money as an opportunity to ask better questions. You will not focus on the lack but instead focus forward on exploiting the resources you do have. You will become more productive. You will innovate. And you will prosper. Necessity truly is the mother of invention.

Plenty of Somethin' from a Whole Lot of Nothin'

In September of 1992, Julie Anderson, an unemployed fine art photographer, got a bright idea: Why not open up a costume rental shop and make some money on Halloween? Julie loved making costumes and had a few hanging around from photo shoots. There was just one problem. Julie had no money for a retail space. In fact, she was just about broke.

Julie made a deal with a swank hotel to rent a room for just one month in exchange for promoting the hotel's Halloween bash. Since she didn't want people to know she had only a few costumes, she put signs up that read "By Appointment Only" and ran an ad in the local weekly. Whenever potential customers called and asked if she had a specific costume, she would ask for their size and then say, "Yes, I have that, but it's rented and won't be back until tomorrow."

Yup. You got it. Julie made each costume to order, staying up all night to finish them before her customers came in for their appointments. She scoured thrift stores, dollar stores, and garage sales for fabric and supplies. With barely any money leftover to eat, her dinner every night was the free nacho buffet at the hotel's bar during happy hour.

By the first of November, Julie had dozens of costumes and a nice stash of cash. Since she loved creating costumes, Julie decided to open shop year-round and launched The Costume Salon. Nine years later she sold her local business – literally thousands of hand-sewn costumes made from found or discounted materials – and opened an online couture costume rental business (www.costumesalon.com).

Today, Julie rents high-end costumes to customers all over the world, designs costumes for films and big-budget plays and musicals, and is regularly featured in magazines such as *American Doll* and *Italian Vogue*. And you know what? Julie still uses the same business model. If she doesn't have it, she makes it, often using discounted or gently-used materials. Julie Anderson is a Toilet Paper Entrepreneur.

Anything for Nothing

If I get one more stinking, whining email about how impossible it is to start a business without any money, I am going to explode. Money, if used wisely, will let you start faster. But lack of money will not prevent you from starting. If you have the ability to send me an email, you clearly have access to a computer or cell phone. More than enough tools to get started. So if you don't have money, stop making excuses and find a way.

Throughout this book I've shared some of my tricks to help you launch and grow your business for little or no cost. (Remember all of those perky little text boxes?) There are a million more. But you're probably thinking free office stuff is all well and good, but I can't start my business until I have enough money to bring my product to market. That is a crock of sheet, if you ask me.

While I agree that you may not be able to produce a fully-realized version of your product design in this very moment, you might be able to introduce a toned down version of it. Maybe you can start with one piece of it. Or maybe you can use something else that already exists and make a simple modification. Or how about performing the service behind the product or for a similar product?

If you still believe you need money, then follow the path of the part-time entrepreneur. Work a job during the day and slowly build your entrepreneurial endeavor at night, or the other way around. There is always a way to achieve, and to do it with little or no money. You just need to believe you can, focus on problem solving, and then DO IT!

If at this point you are still saying you can't launch a company without money, give up. You are just too stubborn and stuck in your limiting beliefs. Until you dissolve The Wall, you will not successfully launch anything.

TPE TIP

Office Furniture – Go to office buildings that have multiple occupants and find out who the landlord or building management company is. Ask them if any businesses are planning on moving in or out in the near future. Then go to these businesses, explain that you heard they are moving, and ask if they will be leaving behind or discarding furniture. Offer to take it off their hands, with a smile.

Sometimes You Need To Borrow

Bootstrapping is the hardest road to travel, but it greatly increases your chances of arriving at the castle a very, very wealthy king. I am a huge believer in surviving on your own, if you can. It forces excellent discipline, and the rewards are greater, but that doesn't mean you should be an idiot.

Starting a company takes guts, persistence, tenacity, and passion, but stupidity is not part of the formula. You need to have some money to live. Your job is not to prove to the world you can make it on your own by becoming homeless. There are times when you might need to borrow cash. There may be other times you have to work at the Burger King just to keep cash coming in – but every other waking hour must be devoted to launching your company, paying back your debts, and driving toward success. Plus you get to eat all those free fries. Yum.

There are a lot of do's and don'ts to debt financing (otherwise known as borrowing.) The traditional methods don't work well. Surprised? I didn't think so.

Bankers Are Anchors

So you need to borrow a full roll of money rather than root through the proverbial wastepaper basket of nontraditional resources? Fine, I'm cool with that. But if you're going to borrow, you better ensure you use the cash to directly grow your fledgling business's bottom line. Don't use it for anything else. Until you have a belief system that maximizes what you have (think three sheets of TP here), you shouldn't borrow a penny. Only when you are able to take a dollar and stretch it a mile should you take in money to fuel your growth.

The first source of money entrepreneurs traditionally think of is bankers. That's the old school approach and is probably the last place you should go. Bankers aren't bad people; they just don't easily understand non-traditional business plans and are risk-averse by nature. Banks are looking for simple, low-risk investments that offer consistent return. They like to get involved with stuff they thoroughly understand and are highly confident will guarantee them a return. A new startup rarely fits the bill.

If you do end up going to a bank, go with a small, local one. They are typically far more aggressive. Ha, ha, that's funny! Aggressive banker. Right. Know this: Bankers are anchors. Many entrepreneurs believe they can only get funding from banks. So when the bank rejects them or gives them unreasonable, shitty terms, these entrepreneurs believe that's the end of it. Bankers keep entrepreneurs anchored, unable to move forward to Plan B.

So if you shouldn't go to the banks, where should you go? The best sources of funding are the people who know you and know your capabilities. Who knows you better than *you*? Nobody! So the first place to borrow money from is you. Now don't cut me off here and say you don't have any money. You might have more than you think. Consider these options:

eBay – Look through the attic, garage, and every crevice of your home. From baseball cards to old toys to your collection of slightly soiled porno mags, somebody wants your crap and will pay good money for it. See what you've got, post it on eBay and get some money in the door. As the old saying kinda goes, "One man's shit is another man's non-shit."

House – If you own a house, consider refinancing and pulling the equity out. If historical trends stay true, your house will continue to increase in value over the long term. Just make sure you can afford the new payment, and avoid frequent refinancing, which may cost you dearly in the long run.

Car – But what if you don't own a house? You may have a car. Did you know you could refinance your car? You can, if you own it. Just be careful. Since cars decrease in value over time, borrowing against them is a financial risk.

401K & IRA – While 401K, IRA, and other investment-account money is intended for retirement, there are situations in which you can borrow from yourself penalty-free. Of course you can just take the money out directly, too, but be aware that you might take a government-induced penalty and tax beat-down.

529 Plan – The 529 plans are intended for college savings but can be freed up for other purposes, too. If you have one, see if you can get the funds out penalty-free. What better education can you get than entrepreneurialism, anyway?

Trade a Paperclip for a House

If you couldn't squeeze enough money out of yourself, it's time to start looking at alternatives. Most will advise you to continue down the funding path of the Four F's: Founder, Family, Friends, and Fools. Per usual, the pundits are wrong. You are the first "F," Ms. (or Mr.) Business Founder, and you can still get cash or supplies of your own accord. Before you run out asking for funds from other sources, try trading up.

Kyle MacDonald proved to the world that he could trade one red paperclip for a house. At the end of one year he not only had his house but a lot of buzz and a book deal.

The story of One Red Paperclip is true, amazing, and a real eye-opener. Kyle started off with a couple basic things (a computer and a paper clip), a simple four-sentence Prosperity Plan, and a variant of a Quarterly Plan, and then backed them up with immediate action. Four simple sentences placed on Craig's List, and Kyle was off to the races. What he accomplished was nothing short of amazing.

"This one red paperclip is currently sitting on my desk next to my computer. I want to trade this one red paperclip with you for something bigger or better, maybe a pen, a spoon, or perhaps a boot. If you promise to make the trade I will come and visit you, wherever you are, to trade. I'm going to make a continuous chain of 'up trades' until I get a house."

With that Kyle was off to the races. All he needed was his natural talent, a computer, a paper clip, and his time. The red paper clip was traded for a pen, which after a few trades became a tool box, and then a generator, which went on to become a snowmobile, and then a box truck, and after a few more trades became an acting role in a movie, which resulted in his Destiny. Fourteen trades and one year later Kyle moved into his new house in the town of Kipling in Saskatchewan, Canada.

Think about what you have to offer that is of value to someone else. Can you provide training, service, or stuff to someone in exchange for something you need? Working with limited resources requires discipline and commitment and is clearly a "harder" path than someone handing you money, but the results can be phenomenal. Shoot, if a paperclip can get you a house, just imagine what you could get for trading this book. Maybe you could have your own island.

Funds from the Folks

After squeezing money out of yourself, your belongings and your skills, it may be necessary to tap the second "F", Family. It's time to raise some cash through Mom, Dad, and your wealthy Uncle Hecklebert. When it comes to borrowing family money there are inherent pros and cons. The upside is that the agreement will probably be quick and will not require lawyers or personal guarantees. The downside is summed up in the word, "probably."

Accepting a loan from a family member is risky because if your business goes sour, things can get ugly fast and last an eternity. Think about all those Thanksgiving dinners where your Uncle Hecklebert recounted the story of how you screwed him, threw a turkey leg at you, and stormed out. Nobody needs that. Nobody.

If you are going to ask the folks for some funding there are a few things to consider. A family loan is just like any other loan, and you need to pay the money back. Unless, of course, your folks just write you a check, pat you on the back, and tell you to take it. In that case give them a big hug and kiss, and get your ass to work. But chances are your family needs money to live, too, so if you agree to a loan, use this little trick to pay it back and sustain a friendly family: Borrow more than you need!

For example, if you need $5K ask for $8K and use the extra $3K to start the payback process on time, or even a little early. This affords you more time to get on your feet and generate revenue. At the same time, it shows your family your commitment to paying the loan back and keeps you in their good graces. As you get in the payback rhythm it will become habitual and easier to pay, and you won't feel like a schmuck.

Sometimes even the best plans don't pan out. If you can't pay back your loan on time or are having any difficulty whatsoever, tell your family lenders as far in advance as possible and work out a new plan to pay the money back. Communication is the key – *and* it could save your Thanksgiving.

TPE TIP

Office Furniture (Part Two) – Root around in thrift stores or at garage sales to find used furniture. The American Cancer Society and other charities have annual garage sales with countless office items, including supplies like reams of paper, extension cords, and ink cartridges. Remember to go on the last day when everything is half-price.

Vendors Have Your Money. Borrow It Back!
(Plus Other Options)

Maybe the folks aren't an option, and you don't have a penny to your name. There are still plenty of options to consider before you start selling off pieces of your budding company. If you are doing at least a little bit of business, you have even more options.

Vendor Loans – Contact vendors and tactfully but passionately tell them your vision, goals, and financial needs. They will have a good understanding of your market and a great understanding of you – and may want to invest in your growth. If they consider you a good client, your vendors may give you very favorable terms, loans, or an equity deal. Chances are if they help you out financially, they are also going to make sure that you are a priority on their list. That can help you. As your business grows, your need for their products and services will increase as well, and you're not about to switch vendors after all they've done for you, are you? Figure out how it can be a win-win, and present your case. At the very least you may get better payment terms on existing orders.

Client Loans – Clients are also a good source of funding, but asking them for money is a little risky. Customers may fear that you are in financial trouble, and you may lose them as clients.

Prepaying Clients – A great way to get money is to offer clients a prepayment or retainer option. Ask them to pay up front at the time they place their order for some or all of the services and products. If it is reasonable and fair, offer them a discount for prepaying.

Sell Receivables and POs – Factoring companies will pay you today for money that is due to you in the future. Do you have some big invoices outstanding with clients that would benefit you if they were collected today, rather than in sixty days? If so, factoring may work. Keep in mind, though, factoring companies are out to make a living, too. They will only take on invoices that they are confident they can collect and will take a pretty large percentage, sometimes paying you only 75% of the total invoice. Factoring companies offer the same deal for purchase orders (POs). So if you really need cash now, once the client commits to using your company and issues a PO, you can go to a factoring company and get the coin right away.

Friends – We already discussed how to raise money from yourself and your family. When it comes to friends, you must treat them just like family. Remember, the consequence of a loan gone bad can run much deeper than just bad debt. This time instead of a turkey leg being thrown your way, it will probably be an empty beer bottle.

Fools – When it comes to the final "F," Fools, I suggest you never borrow from them. I think the term "Fools" is thrown around to be a little cheeky, but they are out there. I don't like to consider this approach, though, since a fool implies a win-lose scenario. Basically you are saying you will get the cash you need from people who are idiots for lending it to you. Either way someone is going to lose. And if your "foolish" lenders lose, it probably won't be pretty for you. Even if you come out OK, I believe in karma; what comes around goes around. Taking money from a fool sets you up for paybacks someday, somehow. As Mr. T says, I pity the foo'.

Credit Cards – When I launched my first company and needed inventory for clients, I purchased all of it on credit cards. I was able to borrow about $25K through credit cards, even with zero income and a marginal credit history. Here is the trick I used: I signed up for about ten cards and then signed my wife up for ten more. Between the two of us we got $25K of total credit. When I made a purchase I rolled the balance over to new cards at zero interest. Every chance I got I would pay off one card, get the limit raised, and start loading it up again. I closed the other cards. This is not a clean method and not great for your credit history. But it is very easy to get and helped me to access money immediately.

Don't Borrow To Cover Your Mistakes

I nearly destroyed my company by borrowing to death. It wasn't the credit cards; I paid all of those back. It was the bank loans. I borrowed $250K and blew it. One of the biggest mistakes I made was using the money to cover payroll. I gave myself a bloated salary and paid for employees who weren't needed. Finally, when the money ran out, I had to face the truth and cut my salary, fire employees, and get back on track. But I still had a huge amount of debt on my shoulders.

The lesson in this story is that if you are borrowing money to cover your own salary and others', you clearly have too much money going out. At that moment you need to make the hard decision of letting people go. Chances are you could be doing just as much work, or even more, with fewer people. Get rid of those folks (and their salaries) who aren't adding substantially to the bottom line. You are going to have to fire them at some point, so you might as well do it now and give them a little severance so they can find better jobs elsewhere.

If you can't afford salaries, consider hiring subcontractors to do some of the work an employee would do. You'll save the cost of matching social security and Medicare payments, and you'll save on the cost of employee benefits such as health insurance. Just make sure you issue 1099s at the end of the year for eligible contractors, and take out a basic Worker's Comp policy to cover them, just in case.

Also, if you are paying yourself a fat salary that the company needs to borrow to cover, stop! Pay yourself only what the company can afford and only pay that after you have taken your profit first! We'll talk about the Profit First method shortly. For now, just enjoy being overwhelmed with anticipation.

Don't Give Personal Guarantees

I give in! You tried everything else and it didn't work. Now it's time to go to a banker. They better have a good offer or a really hot teller, otherwise I wish you wouldn't go. But if you do seek funding from a bank, and it makes an offer, write it without a personal guarantee (PG). A PG basically says that if you can't pay the loan back, anything that is owned by you legally goes to the bank. Of course if you are a bank, you want to reduce your risk as much as possible, so you sure as hell better get the borrower to sign away his life. Despite this conflict there can be mutual ground. The bank may not require a PG if you can reduce its risk considerably.

The easiest way to eliminate the PG is by lowering the loan amount. There is an old saying in banking – if you can't pay the bank back $100, that's your problem. If you can't pay the bank back $100 *million*, that's their problem. Other methods may include involving a co-signer such as a family member or even a key client. Seek a way, and you may just find it.

TAKE ACTION NOW!

Building on the tips and strategies included in my book, complete the following exercises to create a customized list of resources that could work for your business. This part is really fun and totally addictive. You'll be scavenging with the best of the TPEs in no time!

1. Make a list of EVERYTHING you need for your business that you KNOW you can get for free. Then make a list of everything else you need. Next, use your TPE ingenuity to come up with ways to get THOSE THINGS for free, too.

2. If you just can't get something for nothing, take your list and brainstorm ways you could barter for what you need.

3. If you still need stuff or services that will cost money, identify ways you could get what you need on the cheap.

CHAPTER 9 – A GOOD, SOLID FLOW

"A penny saved is a penny earned."

– Benjamin Franklin

Recently I received a notice congratulating me on donating a gallon of blood. After some Wikipedia research I learned that the human body has slightly over a gallon of blood pumping through it. Clearly, if I gave a gallon of blood in one sitting I would be a goner. Shoot, even if I only donated one-third of my blood (approximately three pints) in one sitting I might suffer some tough consequences. But since I donate one pint of blood at a time, my body hardly misses it and I can donate as frequently as seven times a year and not miss it. Apparently, my donations piled up, and in a very short time I had given a gallon of blood.

Cash is the lifeblood of your business. I think it's hard to argue otherwise. Shouldn't you treat your money like the blood of your business? Just as blood is often required in a medical emergency, a business in fiscal trouble often requires an infusion of capital.

You never know when a patient will need donated blood, but with a pool of easily accessible blood reserves the chance for survival dramatically increases. Sometimes your business problems are predictable, and other times they will blindside the hell out of you. With a supply of easily accessible cash the chance for business survival dramatically increases.

Do you see the value in regularly "donating" business cash flow to your reserves? The best system is to take your profit first. What do I mean by this? Every time money comes into your business, and **I mean every time**, automatically transfer a percentage of that money into a separate account. Just like a pint of blood, a healthy business will hardly feel the withdrawal. In fact, if you do it first, you'll never miss it. I like to call this reserve the Profit First Account (PFA).

How much money can be transferred to the PFA without threatening the health of your business? Most stable companies should be able to post a profit of 10% to 25% after all expenses. So start with a low threshold wherein maybe 5% of every inbound dollar goes to the PFA. Over time, slowly increase the percentage and monitor cash flow closely to see if your business gets woozy. Don't stow away too much money too quickly. Just as donating way too much blood in one sitting is harmful, rapidly draining cash from business operations could cripple or kill your organization. Once you have adjusted expenses and cash outflow to sustain your PFA withdrawals, you will quickly accumulate a tremendous cash reserve.

Should tough times come knocking on your door, and they often do, you will have your PFA to back you up and, if necessary, bail you out. Of course, as your cash reserves grow, they will ultimately be in excess of any imaginable rainy-day needs. At that point you should take portions as an equity distribution. Trust me, it's a real nice way to reward yourself for running a healthy business.

If you've never given blood, I strongly encourage you to do it. There's no question: it saves lives. If you don't currently donate to your company's PFA account, I strongly encourage you to start. There's no question: it saves companies.

Applying the PFA Process to Your Business

As with everything else in your business, your Profit First Account isn't going to happen unless you take action. Start out slow and easy, and build your way up. Here are the steps to take:

1. Research financial trends on Yahoo! Finance to determine what healthy businesses in your industry earn in profit. Calculate industry profits as a percentage of revenue. For example, I studied many service/investment companies and determined that 20% is a healthy profit number and is achievable among the top performing companies in my industry. 20% is my Profit First Percentage (PFP).

   That being said, 20% may be too much money for a young business. So initially, your company may be best served by having 5% of revenue going to the PFA, adjusting contributions to 8% in the following quarter, and 11% in the next and so on. Continue to ratchet up the PFA savings slowly but surely, quarter by quarter, until you are at the optimal amount determined from your research.

2. Establish your PFA so that it's not easy to transfer money out of the account.

3. Immediately transfer your PFP from every deposit made as a result of sales – and I do mean EVERY DEPOSIT – into your PFA.

4. Use the remaining percentage of money deposited to run your company and pay your salary.

5. Distribute 50% of the PFA balance to equity owners (hopefully just you) on a quarterly basis and leave the remaining 50% in the account for backup.

Here are some of the benefits of the PFA:

1. The PFA is always available as a rainy-day fund. But it better be a serious storm. I mean thunder and lightning, and stuff.

2. You will adjust spending and build a healthy business using the money left over after you withdraw the PFP. You'll probably even earn additional profit on the leftover money.

3. The PFA is a simple monitoring system. Once you have an established PFA for a year or so, you can watch the trend of the PFA at distribution time. If the PFA is growing, so is your business. If the PFA is flat or going down, so is your business.

4. A company that shows a consistent or increasing profit quarter after quarter is much more valuable to a prospective buyer. And you want this, since when you sell your company is when you make some REAL money.

5. The PFA is a way to get big lines of credit. The more you have stashed away, the more lenders are willing to lend. Good luck trying to get a bank line of credit if you don't have any money. But as your PFA grows and banks know you have cash, they will gladly offer you lines of credit, and so will others. Consider your line of credit as a second rainy-day fund.

This PFA plan is simple, and it works, but make sure you avoid the stumbling blocks:

1. If the money in the PFA is easy to take out, it's tempting to "borrow" from it and screw it up. The money MUST be secure and not easily accessible. To address this, team up with someone whom you trust and will hold you accountable. Have her co-sign on your PFA account. Set it up so that your co-signer cannot withdraw money, but both of you need to sign a check in order for *you* to take money out. Similar to how two people must turn a key to release a nuclear missile. Just like that.

2. PFA'ing too much money too fast can be a drain on your company. A lot of people get too gung-ho about this system and start taking the goal PFP – not the starting PFP – immediately and then give up when their company has no money for expenses. The fix is to start now, but to start slow – give yourself and your business time to adjust to the PFA by starting with a small PFP, even if it is just 1%.

3. Believe it or not, PFA money grows quickly. Within a few years the account can actually grow so much that it becomes a risk should there be a lawsuit or some other crisis. If you are in this position, be grateful! Then, on an annual basis, talk with your attorney and your accountant and determine how much of your PFA you should cash out or spend. You could use it to make a major purchase, for example, or it could be your personal year-end bonus – it *is* nice being the owner! Try to strike a balance between legal protections, business asset reduction and keeping enough in the coffers should a disaster strike.

4. Pushing profitability forces slower growth, since that money can't be used to invest in marketing or sales. The discipline of having profit from day one greatly outweighs the "loss" of faster growth. With the PFA, you are assuring your wealth; by growing fast, you are gambling on wealth. I suggest you don't gamble.

5. For goodness sake, make sure you put your PFA in an interest-bearing account! Don't just put it in a checking account. You are putting this money away for quite a while. Have it work for you, not go on vacation. Put it into a money market or other stable interesting-bearing liquid investment.

TPE TIP

Free Workforce – Cricket Hill Brewing Company in Fairfield, New Jersey, has "beer packing parties" wherein a huge line of volunteers pack boxes in exchange for beer sampling. It is fun, and the work gets done. Plus, the "workforce" often walks out and buys a case or two of the beers they had packed.

TAKE ACTION NOW!

Completing the next three steps could save your business and make your life. NOT doing it will put your business in jeopardy and completely stress you out. So just do it!

1. Using the method outlined in this chapter, calculate your goal Profit First Percentage (PFP).

2. Identify a starting PFP that you can easily manage. Most people start around 5% and go up from there until they reach their goal PFP.

3. Set up an interest-bearing Profit First Account (PFA) and start funneling your starter PFP into the account with each and every deposit.

CHAPTER 10 - KEEP YOUR BUSINESS TO YOURSELF

"A fool and his equity are soon parted."

– Me

So you have a brand new business that is not worth anything yet, right? Your company is far from generating revenue; you don't have a single client, let alone a phone system to receive calls. It's just a baby! So why not give your best friend some equity now? After all, it ain't worth nuttin'!

If you have or plan to have a child, would you give a portion of your parental rights to your friend, your neighbor or the doctor at the local hospital? I hope you're thinking NO FREAKING WAY. It's your kid for God's sake! Your kid, Jeez!

A child requires a tremendous amount of your time to feed, nurture, train, and keep healthy so he'll stop puking on you. But watching your kid grow is MORE than worth it. Guess what, Chiefy? Your business is YOUR baby! While it doesn't look like much now you will be putting a tremendous amount of time, tears, and sweat into it. As with a baby, you will need to feed and nurture your business, keep it healthy, and teach it not to vomit on you. As your newborn business grows, it will slowly but surely turn into a strong, healthy young adult. It would be a shame for you to do all that grueling work only to be sharing the parental rights when the business starts hitting its stride. So don't do it – don't give your baby away.

Most partnerships fail. Some end in a bitter, emotional corporate divorce, some end with stunted progress, and a few others end with a handshake and smile. I can already hear your argument. "If I am the parent, wouldn't it be better if I had a spouse to help me care for my baby? Wouldn't it be better to have someone to help change the diapers?" I would say yes, if you were really going to have a child. In that case a good solid partnership is critical. But you are starting a company, not having a real baby, so don't get married to equity partners.

Growing a business and parenting have many similarities, but one of the biggest differentiators is that your business can hire many "spouses" to help you feed and grow the corporate baby. There are many ways to bring in extraordinary people and compensate them without sacrificing equity. Treating people well, as you would want to be treated, enables you to create situations wherein both you and the other "guardians" building the company are compensated in a way that does not include equity.

Partners Without Equity

I don't care how close you are to the other person, how well you know her, or even if she is your twin – people are different. Differences are a good thing when it comes to building a company, but small differences can be a big issue with multiple leaders at the top.

Different Perceptions of Risk – Launching a business is risky, no question. It requires serious head preparation, an enabling belief system and a crystal clear vision. Danger lurks if you and your partners go in with different beliefs about the risks involved. Contrary beliefs are limiting and damaging. For example, one partner may be so skittish she calls it quits too early, and the other may be so bullheaded he becomes a dead man walking.

Too Much of a Good Thing – Variety is good when it comes to building a team, but you can't win a game with only quarterbacks. When you add the variable of another leader, the vision can be slightly different, the beliefs may vary and the focus can go askew. As long as the company's progress is consistent with the collective partners' desires, things are good. But when things go off track, watch out. Egos can overtake ethics, pissy-ness can kill passion, and selfishness can destroy success.

Different Immutable Laws – A lot of people go into business with someone they know simply because they know them and the path ahead seems less scary with a partner. Good acquaintanceship doesn't make for a good partnership. For your business to succeed, you and your partner must share the same Immutable Laws and have complementary talents and strengths.

Different Levels of Energy – We all have varying levels of energy, and opinions about our own energy levels in comparison to those of others. One partner who happily works through the night may consider the other lazy for leaving work in time for dinner. The partner leaving at 5 p.m. after all of her work is done may consider her night-owl partner inefficient and distracted. What may seem like a balance in the beginning may lead to serious conflict later on.

Conflicting Vision – A markedly different vision very often divides partners. Going in, everyone says he wants to have a multi-million dollar company, but as time passes, complacency can kick in. The vision of a large company may be offset by the work demands of growing a business. When varying visions stop sharing a common path, problems arise, and things can get nasty.

As you build your company, your biggest investment will be your time, and I can guarantee that no one in your business is going to invest as much time in your business as you; nor will anyone have the same impact as you. Your company may not look like much now, but it doesn't matter where you are now. All that matters is your Prosperity Plan, your Destiny. How big do you envision your business becoming? When it achieves these goals, do you want to share the rewards with other equity partners, even if they didn't work as hard or weren't as smart or didn't bring value to your business?

If you give or sell equity to someone, you have to be absolutely convinced it will grow the company. In many cases you keep half of the company but end up doing triple the work. Triple? Yep. You'll do three times the work partly because you have to spend time fixing problems and differences with the other partners. At the early stages of starting your business it's tempting to undervalue yourself and your company, particularly if it brings in people who show great initial value and expertise. But do you want them to be driving the train alongside you or riding in preferred seating?

Watch Out for VIPs (Very Inordinately Paid Specialists)

Don't give away equity or lots of money to bring in VIPs. VIPs are perceived to be of tremendous value because they have big names, or add credibility to your company, or have key contacts, or bring some other value to the table. More often than not, however, they don't deliver. It's simple, really. VIPs don't deliver because they don't have to. They receive the reward (money or equity) before doing *anything*. Think about it. Would you have started a business if you were already receiving the money, success, and effect that you want to achieve? Probably not.

Know that for your business, you are the VIP. It's your blood, sweat, and tears, damn it, and for that you should be rewarded, not some freeloadin' VIP.

Ideas Are Worth the Time Spent on Them

New business ideas are easy to think up and even easier to dream about. The next big thing is only a couple of beers, a few friends, and thirty-five minutes away. And it's right there at the bar where the equity distribution is discussed. One-third all the way around, man! We're all gonna be rich. Another round of Milwaukee's Best! On me! If you are the schmoe who then puts the majority of effort into getting the idea off the ground, you have just given away the farm.

Ideas don't make money, effort does. Some ideas require a tremendous amount of effort and time. Think cool invention, working prototype, patent and salivating customer base. Add monumental effort and hard work, and your business may be worth something.

Gauge the value of your idea on the effort, not on the idea alone.

TPE TIP

Free Press – Here is the big tip: Start local and small and then build your way up. Your local paper is starving for good stories about local heroes. Email or fax a quick press release, and you'll be surprised how fast the local guys call for an interview or to confirm facts.

Angels and VCs Suck (Kinda)

Let me preface this by telling you that I am a little bitter here – I have dealt with VCs and Angels and I did *not* have a pretty experience. Not all Angels (high-net-worth individuals who invest in businesses) are bad and not all VCs (venture capitalists) suck. They did bring us Google, Starbucks, and other super-successes, after all.

But let's get real here. VCs and Angels are putting money in your business as an investment. They fully want and expect to get a significant return, and fast. They are NOT philanthropists; they are in the business of making money. I'm not saying that these are bad people or even that there is no value in working with them; you just need to have absolute clarity about what their objective is.

Have you ever bought stock in a public company, maybe on the NYSE or NASDAQ? What mattered to you most? That the stock went up, and quick, right? Your goal was to sell quickly for big gains. Right?

Did you care about the cohesiveness of the management team or employee morale? Were you concerned about the personal fiscal health of the top decision makers? Did you wonder if the President had enough time to make it to the family reunion that weekend? Hell no! That stuff probably never, ever even crossed your mind. Your goal was to invest, make good money, and get out. That is the behavior of 98% of the VCs and Angels out there.

While there are a few differences between VCs /Angels and a stock investment, one is significant. When you buy stock there are thousands and thousands of other investors in there with you. Effectively, you spread your risk with others. You all want the company to succeed, but if it fails you all go down together.

Angels and VCs invest with two or three others, not thousands. Hence, their risk is magnified. They are investing in a startup company (risky) and they are going it alone or nearly alone (even riskier). With this level of risk, VCs and Angels have a serious interest in the success of your company, so they don't just give you money, sit back and watch. They often take control, too.

So if you go the VC/Angel route, know that you are an investment, not a partner. And if they don't like how things are going, they will take control (and not give it back) .

There is an appropriate time to consider seeking out VCs and Angels, though, and this is typically once you are already bringing in millions in revenue. At a certain point your growth can be rapidly boosted through an injection of money. That's when you should consider this type of investor. I suggest that you approach Angels after you are in the millions and VCs when you are in the tens of millions. At that point you may be very happy with how things are going and may even consider being your own angel.

The Right Way To Balance Equity & Partnering

Are you still convinced that you can't go it alone, that you will be more successful with the right partner? You may be right. It worked for Sergey Brin and Larry Page. Here are the right ways to choose a partner for your business:

Rather than go in 50/50, let the partner who is performing at the highest level have the majority of the company. Performance-based equity distribution motivates both partners to work hard and creatively for the success of the company and rewards the partner that excels.

Determine specific metrics and critical goals for the company's growth. These may include sales volume, billable hours worked, purchase savings, customer feedback and products/services developed. Have at least three performance variables but no more than five. Then, every quarter for the next two and a half years, review the achievements and split 10% of the equity. At the end of these ten quarters the entire 100% of company equity will be assigned, and the partners will be fairly rewarded for their contribution to the overall success.

It's a Big Deal To Be Small

Partner or not, funded or not, you will start small. This is a very, very big deal. And you can use it to grow big.

Would you call Wal-Mart an intimate experience? Not at all! It is sterile to say the least and, in my opinion, a little creepy. It seems like it ships the same weird-looking, funky-smelling, sweatpants-wearing customers from store to store. But the prices are CHEAP, so I still go often (and get out quickly).

The mega-stores and mega-businesses have an important place in the business world, but they don't have the only place. It is a big deal being a small business. The world needs you. Actually, the world starves for you. The number-crunching mega-store machine can't match the intimacy and nimbleness of a small business, nor its ability to make every single client feel important. This is your advantage in being small, and you need to exploit it big time.

Not Much to Lose – Think about it: you have very little to lose. This is quite possibly your biggest advantage. If an idea has potential you'll go for it because you've got nothing to protect.

The Underdog – Everyone loves to root for the underdog. Take college football. The nation went crazy over Appalachian State's win over Michigan (except for Michigan fans) during the first week of the 2007/2008 season because the Appalachian State Mountaineers were big-time underdogs. The game was professionally commented on more than any other game in history. Leverage the fact that you're an underdog. People just can't help rooting for you, and word gets out quickly when you pull out the win.

Speed – You can move faster and more nimbly than the big guys. All the red tape, back-stabbing, political games, and bureaucracy that occur at big corporations don't happen within a small company, especially when it is just you. You can make a decision in seconds that will take them days or weeks. You can be in, out, and invoiced before they even return the call. Use speed to your advantage.

It Matters – If you have ten clients and you lose one, that's ten percent of your business. If a mega-store loses one, it doesn't care. It cares about the overall trend. As a nascent startup you not only want to do what is takes to find and keep good clients, you *have* to do what it takes. *Every* client is a big deal, and you must make sure he *feels* like a big deal when doing business with you. If you can pull that off, clients will always choose you over the big guys.

Intimacy – Building on the "it matters" concept, when you are small you have the ability to get to know your clients very well. Some of them may even become personal friends, and others will become key customers. All of your clients should be treated like best friends. Get to know them beyond business. What do they care about? What are they interested in? What do they need? Deep down inside we all want to walk, just like Norm from *Cheers*, into a bar where everyone not only knows our name; they stop, look over, and welcome us in. That level of personal attention will keep 'em coming back.

Break the Rules – The big boys have been around the block so many times that they adhere to rules they no longer need. Some established industries get stuck in the mode of doing things a certain way just because they have always been done that way. A small, nimble competitor like you can identify the industry rules, take what you need, and then break the rest wide open.

TPE TIP

Live Rent-Free – When every penny matters, a TPE gets resourceful. You can have your own house, rent-free. It's called housesitting. Check out caretaker.org or housecarers.com. This can be a match made in heaven for Internet-based businesses that can be run out of the home.

Throw Out the Way It Has Always Been

Tim Ferriss, the author of *The 4-Hour Workweek*, won the Chinese National Kickboxing Championship by breaking the rules. Well, not really by breaking the rules; he actually broke the expectations. He broke the tradition.

On a dare, Tim decided to compete in the kickboxing championship. With only four weeks to prepare for the event, Tim was clearly at a disadvantage against competitors who had been in the league for years. He was facing opponents who had committed their lives to the sport. They were born to win – they were the big guys. Tim was the small guy and didn't have a chance. At least not without breaking, or, in Tim's case, *exploiting* the rules.

Rather than take on the impossible task of achieving the performance and experience levels of the masters, Tim hit the books. He studied the known and not-so-known rules of the league. It was here that he discovered the rule that would bring him victory. If he was able to throw a competitor out of the competition ring three times during a match, the competitor would be disqualified, and the victory would go to Tim. This rule played exactly into Tim's talent, his natural strength in throwing things. This time, he just needed to throw people.

The day of the championship, the masters bowed, boxed, and kicked people. Tim bowed, dodged, and threw people. Tim won. Tim Ferriss is a Toilet Paper Entrepreneur.

TAKE ACTION NOW!

No more exercises. No more pondering. No more psyching yourself up. Your last task is to take one giant leap off the cliff and launch your business (if you haven't done so already).

Show us what you're made of. Join the few, the proud, the Toilet Paper Entrepreneurs!

The Youth (and Young at Heart) Advantage

"The greatest disadvantage of young people today is that they have too many advantages."

- Anonymous

Unless you know the secret to the fountain of youth, you'll only be young once. Milk it for all it's worth. I sure did. I pulled many all-nighters, paid little mind to my "unique" living conditions and plowed ahead with excitement and hope for the future. You can go far on hard work and big dreams, often a hell of a lot farther – and faster – than people with more education and experience.

Resilience – Youth brings an ability to rebound that many people lose as they age (unless they remain young at heart). This resilience allows you to bounce back after defeat and try again, unscathed. The entrepreneurial path is littered with pitfalls and roadblocks; you need the capacity to come back again and again relentlessly.

No False Pretense – How come most curmudgeons are gray-haired folk? Probably because they are pissed at how life turned out and depressed about the lackluster ride ahead of them. The young foresee many more possibilities and great experiences ahead. That old saying is true! As a young person your life IS still ahead of you! The best part is, you can determine just how great a ride it will be. If you are a curmudgeon, your life ain't over yet either, Fella. Make it great ride.

Few Responsibilities – Most young people fresh out of college don't have children and spouses to support. You can put all of your energy into launching your company the right way. This is a HUGE advantage.

Energy – No question, a young person has more energy than an older person. Likewise, a person at any age who is living her passion has tremendous amounts of energy. If you are young AND living your passion you are unstoppable.

No Preconceived Notions – Young people, in general, are far more willing to try something new than older people. Just think about the crazy things you tried in college. No need to share, just think about it and keep that smile to yourself. As we age, we often look back at our younger years and can't believe the crazy things we tried. We become less and less open to risk because of all the fears we've picked up along the way. Be young, be crazy and launch your company now.

Flexible Schedule – You pulled the all-nighters in high school and college and still made it to the keg parties with your friends the next day. Without commitments to your own family, you can exploit the flexibility of the single life. You can party all day and work all night. Or is it the other way around?

Money Isn't a Big Deal – You have been eating Ramen noodles for the last four years; another couple years won't kill you. Since most young folks have yet to experience what it's like to have lots of money, going without wouldn't be much of a hardship. Plus, when you start young and poor, there is only one way to go. Up. Chicken Pork Oriental anyone?

The clock is ticking, and you're getting older. Use these advantages while you have them or someone else will. Tick, tick, tick…

Ivy League or County College – So What!

I don't care how smart you are or how talented you are or what college you went to. When it comes to launching a company, that stuff just doesn't matter. What does matter is how smart you believe you are, how talented you believe you are, how driven you are, how focused you are and how persistent you are.

I have presented at college campuses throughout the U.S., from the Ivy Leagues to the community colleges. Almost every student I meet explains how her education is about mastering certain processes. Fourteen weeks of Accounting 101, sixteen weeks of Investment Strategies, etc. This is important stuff, don't get me wrong, but it sure as hell won't have a significant impact on starting a company. To the contrary, if this is the stuff you worry about when you are starting out, you are doomed. The early days of business are about survival. Classes for cooking on a dime and how to make one cheap suit look like three different, not-so-cheap suits will probably better serve you.

It doesn't matter what your background is or how much education you have; what matters is what you believe you can or can't do. Yes, your background and experience have a great influence on your beliefs. But once you realize you have the right and the ability to change your beliefs, you can achieve whatever you can envision.

So if you are a college dropout, don't sell yourself short. You can achieve the same level of success an Ivy Leaguer can and will most likely pass by those well-educated types in a blink of an eye. Just follow your passion, be relentlessly persistent, and truly, truly believe in yourself. The same applies to Ivy grads. Once college is over, we are all on common footing. The people who believe the most will achieve the most.

TPE TIP

Free Lodging – Need a free place to stay during your travels? Become a couch surfer. Check out globalfeeders. com or hospitalityclub.org for a free place to stay anywhere in the world.

Move In with Your Mom (And Other Painful Thoughts)

If you are a young entrepreneur, you may have good fortune in a supportive mom and dad. If your folks will let you move back home after college, then use this to your advantage as long as you, and they, can stand it. I know you don't want to live with them any more than you have to, but if you bunk with the folks for a year or two after college, you can save some serious coin. Just don't live at home into your 30s or 40s. That is just plain old embarrassing.

Reduce your personal and business expenses by starting your company in the basement or your bedroom. Borrow the car. Use the home phone. And there's nothing better than Mom's home cooking. Besides, it's free! Eat at home and have the leftovers for lunch.

Need part-time staff? Perhaps Uncle George can help with the accounting and Aunt Jane can handle email inquiries. Maybe Mom & Dad can be your office cleaning crew (mine were).

Launching a business is about surviving and doing it intelligently. No, it's not glamorous to have Mommy answering the phone or Uncle George reviewing the books. But it is economical and prudent. Save your money, every cent you can, and use the pennies you have to grow. Live "off the land" as long as you can.

Master Bocce Ball

Too old to move back home, or have another really good reason not to? There is still a way. There is always a way. I found a way when I started my first company. I could have moved home, but it would have been tough since I was engaged and had a child. Try springing that one on the folks.

"Hey Ma! Great news! I just started my first company. Yep, but it gets better. I found the girl of my dreams and we are going to get married. No, no, that's not all. I am going to have a son!!! Would you mind if we all move back home?"

Nope, that wouldn't have worked for any of us, not my folks, my wife, or me. So we needed to find an alternative. And when you have no money, it is amazing what you can do. Within a few short days, my wife had found a retirement complex that welcomed us with open, flabby arms. That's right, an old-age community for people between eighty and dead.

So why choose a retirement community at the tender age of twenty-four? Because we could afford it! Rent was something like $475/month for a two-bedroom. For New Jersey in 1995, that was a great deal; plus, the retirees made some good food. Life was not luxurious, but we managed, and ate a lot of Ramen Noodles and hand-me-down fruitcake. And of course we became masters of Bocce Ball and Pinochle.

If you have the will, there is a way. You may have to eat a little of your pride, but it is worth it, and it builds character. Who knows, maybe you and I can have a no-nonsense Pinochle game one day. Winner gets a coupon for the early-bird special.

Still in School? Graduate Profitably.

When the last final exam is done and the last beer bash concludes, your classmates will trod their way home with the parting words, "See ya next year, bee-aacchh." They are off to enjoy some summer sun and *maybe* get a summer job. You should not follow suit. This is an opportunity to launch a small business, even if it is just for a few months.

Make a product that you can sell, freelance a service you have to offer, do whatever you want that can make money. This is about making some payola and learning the critical parts of starting a company. Plus, you probably will make more than minimum wage and have more fun doing it.

Hold on a minute! What about a polished resume that you can show to a future employer? If you are thinking along those lines, you are reading the wrong book. This is about learning the core principles of running a successful business, and there is no education better than doing it.

But what happens when you have to get back to school? You have options here. You can close up shop, or you may be able to keep your business rolling along. Part-time, of course; you do want to keep up the grades and get a good education. Try to recruit a few people on campus to work for you, but avoid using friends so that you can treat them as beer buddies, not colleagues. This is an opportunity to build your leadership skills and learn to manage a team.

Make the most of your college days. Make a little bit of money and, most importantly, don't forget to PARTY!

Party!

You or your folks laid down some serious cabbage to pay for your college education, and you better take full advantage of it. Go out and party, right now! You heard me. PARTY!

I'm not suggesting you get involved in a booze fest (well, maybe just a few); I'm suggesting you learn how to communicate with others and network. Entrepreneurial success is dependent upon your ability to lead and communicate with people. You are going to be the CEO (Communicator, Energizer & Organizer) of your new business so you better start acting like one.

Use your party time at school to find the people you click with. Investigate what it is about your closest friends that you like. What are the values they share with you, with others? Figure out the best and fastest ways to meet other people who share your values.

Try planning a party (strictly legal, of course) with your friends. Can you set a common vision of how the party will go down? Can you get your friends to not just buy in, but feverishly support you?

How great can you make the party, all with volunteer work? Can you get people to do the PR, the collections and accounting, purchasing, and customer service? This is a great opportunity to learn about your own values, hone your skills, discover your strengths, and learn how you best manage people.

If at the end of the night everyone makes a toast to you and applauds you for a job well done, then congratulations! You have potential to be a great CEO. You also have a backup plan as an events coordinator.

THE NOT-SO-HIDDEN BONUS SECTION

Tom "The Big" Crapper

I t would be a sin not to include the story of Thomas Crapper in this book. I can't think of a more fitting way to use these final pages. Mr. Thomas "The Big" Crapper was an entrepreneur, plumber, purported inventor of the flushing toilet and a guy with the best name ever. I gave him the nickname "The Big." Poetic license.

Although Crapper held nine plumbing patents, none were for the flushing toilet that he is often credited with inventing. Instead, Crapper was a sanitary engineer during the 19th century who ran his own plumbing company and owned many patents. Today, one hundred years later, all over London, you can still see manhole covers emblazoned with his name.

Crapper had an extraordinary entrepreneurial run by any measure. The results were financial fortune and eternal fame. He achieved this by:

1. **Acting As If** – He was a plumber who acted as if he belonged in the big leagues and was treated as if he was already there.

2. **Exploiting Strengths** – He knew the industry, he could close down the deals, and he could sell. Little did he know his name would be his best asset. Crapper is the only entrepreneur in the world who, more than one hundred years after his death, can still say he is number one in the number two business.

3. **Small was Big** – He was a small operation his whole life, but look at the fortune and fame it brought him. He was nimble and jumped on opportunity.

4. **Belief, Focus & Action** – He knew he would succeed. He stuck with his business and stayed acutely focused on what he wanted. Crapper did not quit; he just kept marching forward. His products still line the streets of London. That's what belief, focus, and action will get you.

5. **Toilet Paper Entrepreneur** – Through and through, Crapper was a TPE. He didn't come from a silver-spooned, Media Darling background. He held himself solely accountable for his own success. He exploited a niche. He had strong beliefs, he knew exactly what he wanted, and he got up (or sat down) and did it.

According to *Plumbing & Mechanical Magazine*, Tom Crapper "should best be remembered as a merchant of plumbing products, a terrific salesman, and advertising genius." Technically, the origins of how "crapper" became a synonym for "toilet" are unknown. But you and I both know that it can only be the work of a Toilet Paper Entrepreneur. Thomas Crapper, unquestionably, is a Toilet Paper Entrepreneur.

Are you the next Toilet Paper Entrepreneur? I hope so. Actually I know so, if you know so. So, no more jibber-jabber. There is nothing else to discuss. This is your moment. It's your turn to succeed. You *can* clean up with just three sheets. All you need is to get down to business. NOW!

Made in the USA
Middletown, DE
19 July 2020